Philosophy's
Violent Sacred

Philosophy's Violent Sacred

Heidegger and Nietzsche through Mimetic Theory

Duane Armitage

Michigan State University Press · *East Lansing*

Michigan State University Press
East Lansing, Michigan 48823-5245

LIBRARY OF CONGRESS CATALOGING-IN-PUBLICATION DATA
Names: Armitage, Duane, 1982– author.
Title: Philosophy's violent sacred : Heidegger and Nietzsche through mimetic theory / Duane Armitage.
Description: East Lansing : Michigan State University, 2021. |
Series: Studies in violence, mimesis, and culture | Includes bibliographical references and index.
Identifiers: LCCN 2020010521 | ISBN 978-1-61186-387-1 (paperback) | ISBN 978-1-60917-661-7 (PDF)
| ISBN 978-1-62895-420-3 (ePub) | ISBN 978-1-62896-421-9 (Kindle)
Subjects: LCSH: Girard, René, 1923–2015. | Memetics. | Heidegger, Martin, 1889–1976.
| Nietzsche, Friedrich Wilhelm, 1844–1900.
Classification: LCC B2430.G494 A76 2021 | DDC 194—dc23
LC record available at https://lccn.loc.gov/2020010521

Book design by Charlie Sharp, Sharp Des!gns, East Lansing, Michigan
Cover design by David Drummond, Salamander Design, www.salamanderhill.com
Cover art is *Animals* (1913), by Franz Marc (1880–1916), 39.8 × 45.6 cm, watercolor on paper,
at the Pushkin Museum, Moscow, Russia. Used with permission of Bridgeman Images.

Visit Michigan State University Press at *www.msupress.org*

Contents

Acknowledgments

This book is the fruit of a recent obsession with René Girard's writings, which first began in the summer of 2012 when my mentor and colleague Bill Rowe gifted me one of Girard's books. I am grateful to Bill for his introducing me to Girard and for his constant friendship and support. I am grateful for the countless hours discussing Girard with my Scranton colleagues: Nathan Lefler, Daryl DeMarzio, and Christopher Haw. I am also grateful to my colleague and friend Joel Kemp for his friendship, support, and for putting up with my incessant questions regarding postmodernism and theology. I am grateful to Lizzy Polishan, Thomas Shaffern, Juliana Melara, and Abbey Murphy for being excellent students and conversation partners for Girard and mimetic theory and for their suggestions in revising the manuscript. Finally, I am most thankful for my wife Claire, who read this manuscript many times and who has talked with me daily (and nightly), for months, about Girard.

Introduction

This book attempts a critique of postmodernism and Continental philosophy through the lens of the philosophy and mimetic theory of René Girard. The path taken to achieve this end is one of engagement with the philosophy of Friedrich Nietzsche and Martin Heidegger, both of whom I regard as the foremost representatives of Continental and postmodern thought. It is my contention that Girard's engagement with Heidegger and Nietzsche radically alters many of the axioms of current postmodern, Continental philosophy—in particular the overcoming of metaphysics (Platonism) and ontotheology, on the theoretical level, and, perhaps more importantly, Continental philosophy's tacit commitments to (neo-)Marxism, on the practical level. Thus, I will argue that detailed attention to the implications of Girard's philosophical thought results in a paradigm shift that deals a deadly blow to Continental and postmodern thinking. Finally, I believe Girard's thinking solves the very problems that Continental and postmodern thinking sought (but failed) to solve, namely the problems of violence and victimization, particularly within the context of the aftermath of the Second World War.

Girard's thinking shows that at the heart of postmodern thinking lies an entanglement in what Girard will refer to as the violent sacred. I will argue, by way of Girard—Girard's readings of Nietzsche and Heidegger—that Continental thinking has made a twofold error from which it has nevertheless profited. First, Continental and postmodern thinking has misidentified the source of violence as originating within the Western metaphysical tradition, in particular within reason (*ratio*) itself. Second, it has failed to recognize the Judeo-Christian source of its ethic—the ethic of concern for victims. Instead, I will argue, with Girard, that postmodernism has failed to see that the real origin of violence lies within the mythic sacred and has even, at times, embraced such violence—even quite explicitly in the philosophies of Heidegger and Nietzsche—in its attempts to overcome violence.

All of this of course requires unpacking, and thus will be the focus of the majority of the book. However, in the interest of better framing my argument, I ought first to define what I mean by terms such as "postmodernism" and "Continental philosophy," as I will use these terms, for the most part, interchangeably throughout the text. Moreover, even somewhat obvious terms such as "metaphysics," "Platonism," and even "reason" require definitions, as I will be using these terms in what may initially appear to be a particularly nuanced sense, but nevertheless remains the manner in which they are generally understood within the context of not only Continental philosophy, but the Western philosophical tradition as well, a tradition in which Nietzsche, Heidegger, and Girard were quite versed.

By the term "Continental philosophy" I refer to the philosophical thinking of the nineteenth and twentieth centuries that took place primarily on the European continent, most especially in Germany and France. This philosophical thinking is most influenced and even dominated by Martin Heidegger, who is further indebted to Nietzsche (in particular, Nietzsche's critique of metaphysics) and Edmund Husserl (in particular, Husserl's method of phenomenology). From Nietzsche, Heidegger took his impetus to critique this history of Western philosophy as the history of *metaphysics*, which both Nietzsche and Heidegger understood here primarily as various configurations of Platonism—insofar as Platonism simply "splits the world in two," in terms of a world of appearance and a world of truth (in this sense, then, anyone from Aristotle to Kant would be "Platonist"). I will of course flesh this out within the body of this text. However, it is worth noting (and insisting) that when the terms "Platonism" and "metaphysics" are employed by these thinkers (often synonymously), they mean a very basic understanding of reality in terms of two worlds or spheres.¹ Heidegger, then, following Nietzsche, in his seeking to "overcome metaphysics," is seeking an overcoming of Platonism qua an overcoming of a split-world metaphysics, which includes an overcoming of *reason* (*Logos, ratio*) itself as the dominate "ground" (*Grund*) of reality. I will return momentarily to this point of over-coming reason in the context of postmodernism.

To return briefly to Heidegger's foremost influences: it was from Husserl that Heidegger gleaned his primary training in the philosophical method of phenomenology, which for Husserl meant a return to things themselves as they appear to human consciousness, bracketing out their actual exis-tence. Husserl, however, remained for Heidegger stuck within the Western metaphysical tradition with its overreliance upon *ratio* and the split world. Indeed, Husserl's phenomenological method required a strict step-by-step process in order to discern and ultimately intuit the essence of things, which, for Heidegger ultimately lapsed into the bifurcation characteristic of meta-physics and Platonism. In contrast, Heidegger's phenomenology, which has become the dominant form of phenomenology in Continental circles (if one can even be said to be a "phenomenologist" in such circles anymore), takes the approach of seeking to undercut *ratio* (thereby undercutting metaphys-ics) in order to reveal a deeper and more original experience of "being" (by avoiding essences, or "reasons," in favor of moods attuned to things' appear-ances). Again, the specifics of this process will be addressed within the body of the text. However, it is worth noting at the outset that Heidegger's think-ing remains more influenced by Nietzsche than by Husserl, *insofar as* the question of the primacy and function of reason is concerned.

I noted above that Continental philosophy is quite simply dominated by the thinking of Heidegger. By that I mean that Heidegger's critique of metaphysics, or what Heidegger later referred to as his critique of the "onto-theo-logic" of metaphysics, is simply axiomatic to nearly any and every Continental philosophic endeavor. That is, the assumption, not only that metaphysics leads to ontotheology, but that such metaphysics qua onto-theology is ultimately a failed project, is the presupposition of the majority of Continental thinking (e.g., Richard Kearney, Jean-Luc Marion, John D. Caputo, Jacques Derrida, Levinas, etc.). Heidegger's argument, in short, is essentially that metaphysics, in splitting the world in two—between an intelligible, true world, and an apparent world—ultimately leads to a kind of failed theism, where God becomes the highest ground (cause, being, essence, etc.); for insofar as things are thought of in terms of grounds, such grounds must in turn be grounded, which eventuates in a highest ground, namely God. Thus metaphysics necessitates theism, albeit one where God appears as highest cause within a larger framework of causes, and it is such theism that Continental philosophy contests. This is not to say that Continental thinking is ipso facto atheistic, but rather that it assumes that metaphysical theism is bankrupt, and that such theism leads to various forms of violence, a theme that will be covered extensively in this book.

I do not in any way intend to limit Continental philosophy merely to a Heideggerian critique of metaphysics and ontotheology, but rather simply delimit it within these parameters. Equally important to the essence of Continental philosophy, for example, is the critique of science and scientific reductionism, which has its origins in Husserl, Heidegger, and Nietzsche, but even as far back as Kant and Kierkegaard. That is, Continental philosophers tend also to take as axiomatic the idea that science cannot account for all of human experience, and, moreover, often argue (as did Nietzsche, and Heidegger to some extent) that science ultimately points to the revelation that it has nothing at all to do with *truth*, but rather technology, control, and power. Indeed, it is in terms of this relation between truth and power that Continental thinking often bleeds into postmodernism, and for this reason the terms "Continental philosophy" and "postmodernism," I argue, can often be used interchangeably. It is therefore to the definition(s) of postmodernism that I will now turn.

Postmodernism often refers to the French reception[2] (e.g., Derrida, Foucault, Lyotard, etc.) in the latter half of the twentieth century, of the German philosophy of the late nineteenth and early twentieth centuries (again, Nietzsche and Heidegger predominantly), and it has been perhaps most famously defined by Jean-François Lyotard as a mistrust of "metanarratives."[3] While Lyotard's definition is true, there is perhaps a better way of formulating what precisely it was that French thinkers received from the Germans, which, I think, can quite easily be framed as a *critique of reason*. At its core, postmodernism is a critique, to some degree or another, of reason, rationality, and, ultimately, intelligibility and truth, often in favor of power. It is in terms of this criticism of reason that I will therefore employ the term "postmodernism" throughout this text. Indeed, postmodernism, as I see it, marks essentially the French reception of Heidegger's and Nietzsche's criticisms of reason, and thus what all thinkers of postmodernism have in common is not simply a mistrust of "metanarratives," but a mistrust of reason itself. Consequently, this mistrust of reason extends to truth, and thus to *being* ("isness") itself, since truth is primarily understood in the Western tradition as the correspondence between an idea and reality.

It is worth noting that although perhaps a full-blown critique of reason began much earlier than Nietzsche in the critical philosophy of Immanuel Kant, Kant's critical philosophy in no way intended to get "behind" or "underneath" reason to some supra- or subrational ground. Rather Kant sought merely to delimit reason's proper boundaries (according to Kant, to make room for faith) and to limit reason's and thus knowledge's scope of applicability, mainly to the empirical realm, leaving metaphysical questions to mere dialectical speculation (or faith). In other words, Kant's limiting of reason does not undermine reason, as it is reason itself, for Kant, that performs its own critique. The postmodern project, by contrast, seeks not merely to limit reason, but to get beyond reason to some nonrational foundation.

In sum then, I understand the term *post*modernism to mean *post*rational, or at least an attempt to get beneath or beyond reason to reason's nonrational conditions for possibility. As I just alluded to, the most common nonrational condition for reason, according to many postmodernists, is power. Nietzsche, for example, argued that behind reason's will to truth was simply the will to power, and that the cognitive faculties were mere impositions of static "being" upon the ever-changing flux of becoming. Heidegger took a somewhat more nuanced position, arguing, as we shall see, that the history of Western metaphysics, which begins with Plato, culminates indeed with Nietzschean will to power (as the former's utter reversal), but such will to power as the operative understanding of being in modern science and technology nihilistically *reduces* the meaning of being to a singular meaning so as to control and manipulate it. However, for Heidegger, while behind Western metaphysics and reason lies indeed will to power, a deeper, more primordial reality—what Heidegger calls "beyng" (*das Seyn*)—lies behind and beneath the understanding of being as power. How exactly this plays out in Nietzsche and Heidegger will be the topics of chapters 2 and 3 of the text.

Regardless, the manner in which power functions in relation to reason is of primary concern for postmodernists precisely because it addresses the question of morality. That is, despite postmodernism being a wholescale attack on truth and metatruth of any kind, it nevertheless almost always becomes tied to a general ethic and moral sentiment, to what Girard often calls the Judeo-Christian ethic of "concern for victims," which further gets politized in the political ideology of Marxism. Yet such ethic and political "truths" or "metanarratives" are in obvious tension with postmodernism's wholescale critique of truth and metanarratives. Thus, the obvious question to pose is this: What precisely accounts for this problem? That is, why can postmodernism and Continental philosophy critique truth so radically on the one hand, and on the other fall prey again to various "absolutes"? In this book, I will argue not only that Girard can account for the contradictory tensions inherent in postmodern and Continental thinking, but that mimetic theory can also solve the very problems that postmodernism itself has failed to solve, namely the problems of human violence.

The majority of this text will therefore be devoted to showing how Girard reframes the fundamental issue of Continental and postmodern philosophy—the question of what we could call the "hegemony of reason"—by examining Girard's engagement with Nietzsche and Heidegger. Girard's thinking essentially deconstructs and reconfigures the paradigm set by Nietzsche and Heidegger by uncovering the origin of violence within the mythic sacred and not within the hegemony of reason and Western metaphysics. Given the centrality of Nietzsche and Heidegger to the paradigm itself, any critique of them would itself apply to the subsequent thinkers within Continental philosophy. In short, Girard offers a "critique of the critique" of reason in postmodern, Continental philosophy and shows how such thinking further entrenches itself in the problems it sought to solve. I hope to show, via Girard, not only why the critique of reason, metaphysics, and ontotheology is utterly misplaced, but also why (a return to) ontotheological, metaphysics, and, in the end, Christianity are the only viable options in understanding power and in controlling violence.

It would, however, be impossible to discuss these issues that arise in Nietzsche, Heidegger, and Girard without doing so within the context of Christianity. Obviously, Christianity figures quite prominently in Girard's mimetic theory; but Christianity plays an equally important role in the thinking of Nietzsche and Heidegger. Nietzsche memorably said that Christianity is merely "Platonism for the people," given its palatable packaging of the split-world metaphysics, as well as the necessary prominence it gives to Logos (not only as the second person of the Trinity, but to Logos qua *ratio* as well). Heidegger also thought that Christianity, at least Christianity's conceptual framework, was merely the outer shell of a deeper Platonism, insofar as Christianity became the herald of the very metaphysics of modern science and technology. Both thinkers thus saw Christianity and Platonic metaphysics as inextricably bound and saw this union as foundational to Western culture, and thus aimed a large part of their criticisms at Platonism as Christianity's metaphysical foundation. However, both thinkers offered explicit, outright critiques of Christianity (as a religion and morality) in its own right, apart from its metaphysical foundations. I hope to show, again, why not only both Nietzsche and Heidegger's critiques of Christianity qua Platonism are incorrect, but perhaps more importantly why their criticisms of Christianity as a religious and moral framework also fail. That is, while both thinkers are correct in seeing the intrinsic metaphysical link between Christianity and Platonism, each fails to see (or, in the case of Nietzsche, accept) the unique *religious* contribution of Christianity. In the case of Nietzsche, Christianity is rightly understood as a kind of Platonism, albeit for Nietzsche a watered-down version, but also misunderstood or mischaracterized as a weak and slavish moral perspective laced with resentment, wherein such weakness marks the heart of Western culture's morality. Heidegger, however, largely downplays and even ignores Christianity's religious, cultural, and moral significance, relegating it, again, in essence to a mere outer shell of Platonism. It is with regard to this question of the significance of Christianity, in its religious and moral dimensions, that Girard's mimetic theory, I think, is perhaps most important in identifying fundamental errors in Continental and postmodern thought.

Indeed, Girard and Nietzsche are in complete agreement, over and against Heidegger, as to the centrality of Christianity in the formation of Western culture; the difference lies in whether Christianity's role has been positive or negative. Unfortunately, Heidegger's sense of the relative insignificance of Judeo-Christianity has come to dominate Continental philosophy and, I think, is largely responsible for Continental philosophy's fundamental errors regarding violence and power and the ways in which to understand and remedy them. As I will argue, with Girard, the failure to recognize Christianity's central role in the formation of the West's understanding of both God and morality has itself led to various consequences, including postmodernism and Marxism.

As noted above, essentially both Heidegger and Nietzsche see reason and truth as the real cause behind violence. For Heidegger, reason and truth remain wedded to a certain understanding of being that in the end remains reductionistic and even violent. For Nietzsche, "being" itself is a fiction created by resentment and hatred toward life as an ever-changing state of becoming. Both share the idea that truth, absolute truth, is the problem that leads to nihilism and violence. The goal of the entirety of this book will be to show why exactly this position is false according to Girard's mimetic theory. However, I do not intend here—and Girard's mimetic theory certainly is not—simply a *destruction* of Heidegger, Nietzsche, and Continental thinking altogether, but rather a *deconstruction*; that is, while mimetic theory, in uncovering the *truth* of sacred violence operative in Heidegger and Nietzsche, exposes problematic assumptions and axioms (particularly regarding "truth"), it nevertheless seeks to salvage many insights not only from Heidegger and Nietzsche, but also from the Continental tradition itself.

These introductory remarks thus far have been limited to what I believe are mimetic theory's criticisms of Continental philosophy. However, in this book, I do not intend to simply offer a critique without at the same time putting forth a plausible alterative. The plausible alternative happens to be in this case precisely what Nietzsche and Heidegger were so critical of, namely Christianity and Platonic metaphysics (including ontotheology). That is, in what follows, through Girard's engagement with Nietzsche and Heidegger, I will show how Christian metaphysics, in the context of the insights of mimetic theory, remains the only viable, and more importantly *consistent*, option in the hopes of understanding and curtailing violence and power. Moreover, I will show how ontotheological, Platonic metaphysics and mimetic theory are quite compatible systems, and how such metaphysics remains the only ontology possible given the axioms and conclusions of mimetic theory. Now to be clear, when I argue that Girard's "ontology" implies a Christian Platonism or a Christian metaphysics, I do not mean that Girard understood himself necessarily in those terms (as we shall see, Girard had a rather ambivalent relationship with Platonism proper). Rather, I mean Platonism, or Christian Platonism, in only the most basic sense, the sense employed by both Nietzsche and Heidegger, namely the split-world metaphysics, wherein there exists a true, supersensible, or intelligible world beyond the apparent sensible one. This "Platonism" can therefore cover all manner of configurations, including basic Thomism and Augustinianism. Indeed, it would be difficult to reconcile orthodox Christianity with anything other than Platonism as construed in this most basic sense. I will address in more detail this distinctive use of the term by both Nietzsche and Heidegger; however, what may seem like extremely idiosyncratic uses of terms at the outset are in fact vernacular to those familiar with Nietzsche and Heidegger.

I should also note that I do not assume the reader's in-depth familiarity with any thinker discussed in this book, including René Girard. Thus, chapter 1 is mostly devoted to laying out what I consider to be the basic framework and fundamental insights of mimetic theory, and then beginning to describe what I call an "ontology of mimetic theory." Chapter 2 concerns Nietzsche, specifically Girard's and Heidegger's interpretations of Nietzsche; however, my reading extends beyond both Girard's and Heidegger's, as I attempt to apply mimetic theory to Nietzsche in significantly more detail. In particular, this will involve engaging texts in Nietzsche that Girard did not, as well as applying Girard's insights to Heidegger's understanding of Nietzsche as "the last metaphysician," as one who puts forth a metaphysics of will to power, becoming, and eternal return. I hope to demonstrate in this chapter exactly how Nietzsche's overturning of Platonism devolves into a philosophy that affirms violence. Chapter 3, the longest chapter in the book, is devoted wholly to Heidegger, first laying out basic concepts and terms in Heidegger's lexicon, and then turning to a detailed reading of Girard's engagement with Heidegger and, again, an attempt to further apply mimetic theory to Heidegger in a larger scope than Girard had done. I will attempt to show in this chapter precisely how Heidegger's overcoming of metaphysics and ontotheology becomes a philosophy that, like Nietzsche's, affirms violence. Finally, in chapter 4, I attempt to draw together the insights of mimetic theory gleaned in the previous chapters' discussions of Girard and Nietzsche in order to argue why postmodern, Continental philosophy fails, in its critique of reason and truth, to overcome violence and, moreover, fails to account consistently for its ethic, which, I argue, with Girard, is absolutely Judeo-Christian at its core. Moreover, I argue that postmodernism's "metaphysics" is fundamentally Nietzschean, in terms of will to power, albeit a metaphysics that is coupled with the Judeo-Christian ethic of concern for victims, which in turn creates a strange form of hyper-Christianity that ultimately becomes indistinguishable from Marxism.

CHAPTER 1

The Sacred as Violence

This chapter will serve largely as a summary introduction to Girard's theses on violence and religion, and thus as a propaedeutic toward the philosophical implications, applications, and problems raised by Girard's thinking. It is my contention that Girard's thinking deals a fatal blow to what are considered to be the essential theses of postmodernism, namely postmodernism's critique of rationality, truth, and metanarratives, as well as its self-tethering to Judeo-Christian ethics. However, the reader must first be familiar with Girard's theses and terminology. In what follows, I will attempt then to briefly summarize and distill Girard's thinking into what I consider to be three essential theses or insights, at least as they are relevant here for our philosophical purposes.[1] The theses are as follows: (1) mimetic desire as the necessary constitution or essence of human nature, (2) violence (caused by such mimetic desire) as the essence of the mythic sacred, and (3) Judeo-Christianity's deconstruction of the mythic, violent sacred, and the subsequent ethic that follows from it.[2] Given lack of familiarity with Girard's thought in much of the philosophical community, I seek to lay out here Girard's insights as clearly and as concisely as possible from the entirety of his published works and interviews. For Girard scholars or for those already familiar with his work, the first section of this chapter may appear somewhat unnecessary and even tedious. However, not only will a recap of Girard's essential insights benefit those largely unfamiliar with Girard's work, but it also will better structure a proper discussion of just how radical Girard's insights will prove to be for Continental and postmodern philosophy, especially as these insights affect the ways in which Nietzsche and Heidegger can be read. In the second part of this chapter, I will only briefly begin to discuss such philosophical implications and applications of Girard's thinking, saving such philosophical questions for the next three chapters. Nevertheless, it is important to raise issues as they arise within Girard's thinking in order to best prepare for a proper confrontation with the thinking of postmodernism in Heidegger and Nietzsche.

Girard's Thesis

René Girard's thesis concerning violence and the sacred remains fairly simple: violence is at the heart of religion—the sacred. The sacred is always or was always tethered to violence, in particular *sacrifice.* Whether it be human sacrifice (which Girard thinks was original) or animal sacrifice, the blood of the sacrificial victim is essential to the sacred and its *sacrificial* acts (as the word itself suggests: to make sacred). Yet there remains something fundamentally concealed in the sacred such that its inherent violence has long remained unnoticed.

For Girard, the root of all human violence lies in a key concept: *mimetic desire.* Mimetic desire means simply desires that are imitated from others and thus learned in and through imitation. Thus, in a sense, the root to all *desire* comes not from within, but from without.[3] Desire is mediated through an "other," or what Girard often calls a "model." Humans learn their desires, what or even *whom* to desire, through the desires of others who model such desires.[4] In other words, for Girard all desire is imitative, and desiring occurs *because* someone else desires it.

Girard, following Aristotle, thinks that our deep capacity for mimesis is what makes us distinctly human. Animals indeed have the power to imitate, and there are even mimetic desires among animals, but the capacity for mimesis is far greater, Girard believes, for humans. Now it is, strangely, this very trait that makes us human, *mimesis,* that at the same time also leads to conflict and violence. Why? For Girard the problem lies in the very triadic structure of desire (the subject, the object, and the model) in that it almost always gives way to conflict, or *mimetic rivalry*. The model of the object of my desire soon becomes an obstacle to that very object. Moreover, I myself become an obstacle, a *skandalon,* to my model's desire of the same object, as he will likely desire the object more now than I too desire it. Rivalry inevitably ensues.[5]

Thus for Girard humans are fated to violence by their very mimetic nature, as such nature tends to eventuate in rivalry and conflict. Human beings learn their desires from each other, mimetically, and such mimetic desires lead to violence, in part, due to the scarcity of physical objects, but even more so because, in the end, desire is not, for Girard, about the object(s) desired, but about those *who* desire them; that is, I seek (desire) ultimately to possess the other who models my desire (Girard names such desire to possess not the object but the person, *metaphysical* desire).[6] Regardless, human communities always and inevitably become violent. The question becomes then, for Girard, how have human beings evolved in order to cope with their inevitable violence? That is, how have human communities survived this long without destroying themselves (due to their mimetic nature)? For Girard, the answer is *religion.*

According to Girard, religion functions as a cathartic mechanism through which the human community can, so to speak, "let off steam" and channel its pent up frustrations and hatred (born of mimetic rivalry) toward a single individual who is then collectively persecuted by the community qua the collective mob. It is essential that the community sees this single individual as the cause of all of prior communal strife; that is, the individual must be considered *guilty,* and even *evil,* and must therefore be purged from the community in order, so the community thinks, to rid itself of this violent contagion (e.g., Oedipus's sins of incest and fratricide are causally linked to the plague in Thebes). The guilty victim allows for communal unification in the name of justice and the banishment the evil, and from such unification via collective persecution a *cathartic peace* is achieved. The community is bonded together over and against the single individual such that harmony is restored to the once-rivalrous and strife-laden community (e.g., peace returns to Thebes once Oedipus is banished or blinds himself). For Girard, this tells us something striking about human beings, namely that the main foundation of intersubjective, communal experience lies in *persecuting,* in *victimizing.*[7] Humans feel united collectively in their victimizing, which explains nicely why human beings continually gravitate toward the mob phenomena, even in modernity (certainly in modern politics).

Thus the victim for Girard is a kind of *pharmakon*—a poison and a remedy. The victim, originally perceived to be the very cause of all of the community's evil, is later, due to the collective peace that ensues, deified. Thus, Girard can write, "The peoples of the world do not invent their gods. They deify their victims."[8] These deified victims are those around whom mythology and ritual sacrifice revolve, insofar as such myths and rituals reenact victims' original persecutions via the mob.[9] Every ritual, every sacrifice, and every mythic tragedy recollects (unconsciously, of course) a founding persecution and victimization of one who was deemed guilty, but later revealed to be divine.[10] Thus for Girard violence *is,* in a very real sense, the "sacred." That is, the sacred necessitates fear and awe precisely because of its confluence with violence. Ritual sacrifice then keeps human violence "in check." This sacrificial mechanism, for Girard, is essential to not only the formation, but also the continuation of any and every culture. Ritual sacrifices in effect prevent further violence from extreme escalation. According to Girard, this logic of sacrifice makes little sense outside of a proper understanding of the founding murder, the founding victimization. Yet, for Girard, the real logic to sacrifice remains *concealed* to those who offer it.

In early mythology and ritual, the fact that the previously perceived "guilty" victim was later regarded as divine, demonstrates that there was indeed a moral *complexity* to the gods and the sacred. That is, gods did not have to be morally perfect; in fact, gods, for example, Dionysus, are often instigators of havoc. Furthermore, the rituals that recall the founding death of the now-god always, for Girard, at least originally, contain a reenactment of that sacrifice. Thus, these rituals originally must have included human sacrifice. It is only later, Girard argues, that animal sacrifice came to substitute, with less cathartic effect.[11] Regardless, cross-culturally, Girard discovers that ritual is continually bound together with sacrificial acts, usually demanded by the god(s). Thus notions of propitiation and atonement arise, wherein the gods continually need blood in order to "appease" and avert their wrath, wrath directed at the community. In other words, unconsciously this wrath is nothing other than the wrath within human beings, who, were it not for a continual reenacting of the founding murder, would continue to allow their violent and rivalrous urges to escalate. Sacrifice thus keeps human violence checked.

The recollection of the violent sacred that is reenacted in ritual is called *myth*. However, for Girard, the most crucial element of myth is not simply that it is the recounting of victimization, but that it is a recounting *from the mob's perspective*. That is, myth is the recollection of the death of a victim from the perspective of the persecutors. What if, however, a "myth" were to be told, not from the persecutors' perspective, but rather the victims'? What would an inverted mythical account of sacrifice look like? For Girard, the Judeo-Christian tradition, beginning with the Hebrew Bible and culminating in the Passion of Jesus exemplifies this inversion, and even deconstruction, of myth. The victim's perspective *deconstructs* myth precisely due to the revelation that the victims of sacrifices were never guilty, but rather always *innocent*. This innocence remained wholly *concealed* from mythical accounts of the sacred, and the biblical tradition begins to reveal such concealment and thus reveals what Girard refers to simply as the *scapegoat mechanism*.

For Girard, victims, all victims, are *always* innocent scapegoats. This much is revealed by Judeo-Christianity. Indeed in the Bible, both the scapegoating of the innocent, as well as the mimetic rivalry due to envy, are precisely made explicit. Examples include the story of Joseph, who is victimized by his brothers due to their envy, and who is punished for resisting of Potiphar's wife (which Girard reads as an inverted deconstruction of Oedipus), and Cain's murder of Abel, who was murdered because "his own deeds were evil, and his brother's righteous" (1 John 3:12). The Jewish people themselves, through their continual persecution, represent a constant reminder of the scapegoating of the innocent. The Gospels present Jesus as the scapegoat par excellence, the innocent victim of a collective mob; indeed the Gospels speak consciously about scapegoating and therefore ipso facto deconstruct it (for scapegoating is contingent, for Girard, upon its own concealment). Girard even reads the budding friendship between Pilate and Herod, who are said "to have become friends on that very day" as indicative of the scapegoat mechanism's ability to unify otherwise opposed parties (Luke 23:12).[12] Moreover, we see also the power of the mimetically contagious mob, so powerful that it overtakes Peter to side with the mob in denying and victimizing Christ. Girard in sum writes,

To summarize the main point about the Bible and mythology: in the myths an irresistible contagion compels the unanimous communities to see their victims first as guilty and later as divine. The divine stems from the deceptive unanimity of persecution. In the Bible, by contrast, the confusion of the victimization process and the divine is dissolved and gives way to an absolute separation of the two.[13]

In other words, for Girard the Bible represents the beginning of the end of mythology, as it is the absolute antithesis to mythology. Furthermore the Bible exposes the singular lie of mythology: the victim as guilty. Rather, in reality, the victim is *always* innocent. There are no guilty victims, only innocent ones; it is rather the mob that is guilty. This truth remains concealed from mythology, as does the essential scapegoat mechanism inherent in religion, and to the very notion of the sacred. In Judaism however, a new ethic emerges, namely one of *concern for victims.* Compassion and mercy come to the fore, over and against pagan virtues that often exhibit the strength and power of the hero.[14] Only a myth told from the victims' perspective, which is no longer a myth, but an antimyth, in effect, could lead to such emphases upon mercy, compassion, and concern for victims, for "the poor, the orphan and the widow." This Judaic ethic of concern for victims is universalized and spreads to the entire Western world by way of Christianity. For Girard this universalization and dissemination of the Jewish ethic is the single greatest event in shaping Western culture.[15]

Girard considers this movement from mythic persecution to their Judaic inversion as a *desacralization* in the nonpejorative sense. That is, the Jewish tradition begins slowly to deconstruct violence from the sacred; Girard refers often to such a deconstructed, nonviolent sacred as the *holy.*[16] However, for Girard, Judaism's beginning of the deconstruction of the scapegoat mechanism is only that, a beginning, as even within the Hebrew Bible there remain remnants of the mythic or violent sacred.[17] Desacralization is then the slow, progressive revelation of the mythic scapegoat mechanism in favor of nonviolence, in particular, a revelation of the nature of the holy itself as well as a nonviolent ethic. But the climax of such revelation of this nonviolent holy comes, for Girard, through the Passion of Jesus. In Jesus's Passion the victim mechanism of mythological scapegoating is fully unveiled.

The Gospels present the innocent victim, who is God himself (even prior to his death), violently rejected by the collective mob. Indeed, the Gospels are fully self-aware of Christ's innocence, as well as the mob's guilt.[18] Only the Gospels can talk consciously about scapegoating, for "to have a scapegoat is to be unaware that you have a scapegoat."[19] Christianity is therefore, for Girard, the end of myth itself. Human beings, not God, are revealed to be the cause of violence, as the crucified God is a reflective image to human beings of their own violence.

Therefore God can no longer be confused with violence, for Christ dies forgiving his own victimizers.[20] The resurrected Christ does not return at the resurrection with vengeance, but rather "peace" (e.g., John 20:19). Girard writes, "The God of Christianity isn't the violent God of archaic religion, but the non-violent God who willingly becomes a victim in order to free us from our violence."[21] In other words, Girard remains highly critical of any interpretation of Christ's death as a *sacrifice,* that is, one that would make God the Father the agent in Christ's death rather than human beings.[22] Rather than God committing filicide, human beings commit *Deicide.* Why? Because of the escalation of the mimetic contagion wrought by mimetic rivalry that thus demanded a scapegoat victim to restore stability to the otherwise chaotic and destabilized community. God, in Christ, absorbs the violence of community in the guise of the collective mob by willingly accepting the scapegoat role, and, in doing so, unveils publicly the truth of the scapegoat mechanism and, in turn, divulges the truth of human beings in their collective violent nature.

In short then, Christ's death (and resurrection) serve a twofold revelatory role in that it ultimately reveals *both* the nature of human beings and also the nature of God himself. Christ's Passion shows that human violence and its scapegoating are hidden in mythic sacrifice. But more importantly, for Girard, Christ's Passion discloses the essence of God as wholly nonviolent. Rather God takes upon himself humanity's violence in its entirety. As Raymund Schwager writes,

> If even the greatest misdeed against his own Son provoked no reaction of revenge, then there is no other thinkable deed which God would not willingly forgive. His goodness and his forgiveness are shown to be unlimited, because they have expressly stepped over the last recognizable limit.[23]

In other words, God does not respond to human beings' violence with violence, but with love, forgiving his murderers and thereby absorbing their hatred. Moreover, human beings are challenged with the task of imitating this ethic, namely to "resist not evil" but "turn the other cheek" so as to "be like [their Father] in Heaven."[24]

Moreover, Christianity insists upon Christ's, God's, identification with victims (e.g., in Paul's Damascus conversions the risen Christ asks, "why do you persecute *me*?"),[25] and thus Girard thinks it no longer remains possible, post-Christianity, to see victims as guilty, that is, to mythologize them. All victims are revealed to be innocent. Furthermore, not only are all victims innocent, but all *persecutors* are as well, insofar as they are ignorant ("they know not what they do") and thus, in a sense, innocent.[26] For Girard, all violence, especially collective, mob violence, is perpetrated under the veil of ignorance. Girard then follows Plato in believing that evil is always chosen *sub bonum,* under the aspect of good. Evil is always done, by the mob, in the name of "justice." Except now, with the resurrection of Christ, it becomes impossible for this ignorance to remain, as victims are no longer mythologized, but rather vindicated as innocent.

Interestingly, this vindication of the innocent victim is, for Girard, tantamount to the "fall" of Satan, insofar as Girard understands Satan to be the *personification* of mimetic rivalry that eventuates in the accusation of an innocent scapegoat.[27] In other words, "Satan" stands for the violent sacred in its entirety. Girard harkens back to the etymology of "Satan" as "the accuser," as well as the Greek *diabolos,* which means an obstacle (*skandolon*) thrown in the way.[28] That is, Satan is the seducer who seduces humans to mimetic desire and rivalry wherein the mimetic models later become insurmountable obstacles, scandals, that necessitate collective violence for the mimetic contagion, built up from such obstacles, to be purged. Satan therefore "casts out Satan," under the guise of the "powers and principalities" of this world that contain and control violence *by way of violence.*[29] Satan quite simply then is violence itself.[30] Most importantly, in his role as violence, Satan *accuses.* Satan, as the accuser, is therefore the opposition to the *Paraclete,* a term used in the New Testament to refer to both Christ and the Holy Spirit.[31] *Paracletos* (literally "called to the side") for Girard is a legal metaphor of a defender of the accused in law court, which is why the term is often translated as "advocate" or "counselor."[32] The Paraclete is then, for Girard, *the* defender of innocent victims. Myth therefore, which we can now say for Girard is quite simply "Satanic," accuses innocent victims, whereas the Gospels defend these victims.[33] All accusations against victims, even guilty ones, come from Satan as the prince of this world and the instigator of violence and condemnation. Christians, therefore, do not "fight injustice," save by nonviolence, for violence remains perpetually diabolical in nature.[34]

Girard's insistence on nonviolence is an undoubtedly controversial position, but one in fact advocated by Christ.[35] The Judeo-Christian ethic of concern for victims, then, must be coupled with the concession of allowing oneself to be unjustly scapegoated, not returning "evil for evil," but rather absorbing the evil, so as to imitate Christ, who in turn imitates God. Real "exorcism" of evil then is tantamount to an absolute submission to violence.[36]

Philosophical Implications

A discussion of Girard's critique of violence brings us to the heart of Girard's mimetic ethics, namely the *imitatio Christi* and subsequently the philosophic implications of Girard's theory.[37] For Girard, Christ is the perfect model to imitate, since he is not competitive; Christ is not rivalrous and thus will not and cannot become a *skandalon,* a model-obstacle to another in mimesis. Rather Christ imitates the Father, and this is a positive form of imitation rather than a rivalrous one, since the Father and the Son exist in nonrivalrous imitation—"The Son does nothing of his own, but only what he sees the Father doing, for whatever the Father does, the Son imitates" (John 5:19). Furthermore, since the Father does not repay evil with evil, but rather, like Jesus, loves his enemies and is "kind to the ungrateful and the wicked" (Luke 6:35), imitating Jesus then demands one "drop out," so to speak, of any and all competitive relations; otherwise, in repaying evil with evil, or even resisting the evil person, one winds up *imitating* the violence one seeks to overcome. Girard therefore writes,

> *If you want to put an end to mimetic rivalry, give way completely to your rival.* You nip rivalry in the bud . . . if someone is making excessive demands on you, he's already involved in mimetic rivalry, [and] he expects you to participate in the escalation. So to put a stop to it, the only means is to do

the opposite of what escalation calls for: meet the excessive demands twice over. If you've been told to walk a mile, walk two; if you've been hit on the left check offer up the right.[38]

Humans who wish to imitate Christ then must imitate Christ's Passion, by which Christ forgives his enemies and absorbs the evil, for to reciprocate is engage in violent and rivalrous mimesis: "If you resist evil, you are in evil . . . you do what evil invites you to do."[39] Rather, Christians ought to compel their rival to imitate them, and thus compel the rival toward positive imitation.[40]

For these reasons then Girard argues that the Gospels are the only texts that truly recognize the mimetic character of all human relations.[41] Christ asks his imitators to drop out of the mimetic competition, to turn the other cheek, to not resist evil, not only because of some overly sentimentalized love, but rather because Christ understands human beings and their incessant mimetic nature. The only way to "conquer" evil is to stop seeking to conquer it. The only way to resist evil is to not resist it. Instead, one is to desire for the other what you desire for yourself; this is the radicality of Christ's Golden Rule. Girard notes that wherever this positive imitative desire is present, so too is divine grace.[42]

Mimetic desire in itself is therefore, for Girard, not bad—rather, only a certain kind of mimetic desire, namely the kind that leads to mimetic rivalry. Yet what kind of mimetic desire is it that leads to rivalry? For Girard, at least initially, it is a desire for the physical, rather than the immaterial or the spiritual, a point quite familiar to Plato. For Plato, in his "mimetic ontology" of the *Republic* (509–511), one is to desire and therefore emulate the immaterial or meta-physical forms, for example, of the good, the just, the virtuous, and so on. Now ultimately for Plato this imitation of the immaterial begins in knowledge, or at least a kind of intuitive vision of the form. But, in the end, the result is nothing other than imitation. One is to see the form of justice, for example, and become that form. Moreover, a unique quality of the forms as immaterial realities is that there is no need to be competitive over them, for they are not finite, as are physical objects. That is, physical objects can become scarce, since there remains only a limited quantity. Thus desire for physical objects via mimetic desire will escalate to the point of rivalries precisely because there is not enough. Unlike physical objects, the forms engender, then, absolutely no competition, and thus with the forms there is no threat of violence. Indeed in the *imitatio Christi*, Christ's love, like the Father's, is not exclusive, but radically inclusive and thus cannot provoke rivalries. Thus, Christ can make the criteria for imitating him his very own imitation of God.[43] Mimetic desire therefore is a kind of *pharmakon*, a remedy and a poison, depending upon which direction desire imitates. Akin to Buddhist teaching, then, Girard advocates the revocation of a certain kind of mimetic desire, one that desires the physical rather than the intelligible or spiritual, albeit in a certain qualified sense.[44] However, unlike in Buddhism, Girard promotes a positive desire, and therefore a positive imitation that is ultimately for God. It is for this reason, namely the desire to imitate the transcendent, that Socrates is a kind of proto-Christ figure, who suffers unjustly as the innocent victim, as his desire for the "other world" provoked an envy that ultimately led to his demise.

Girard's promotion of a kind of quasi-Platonic mimesis could not be more at odds with the postmodernism of Nietzsche and Heidegger. Both Nietzsche and Heidegger argue, as we shall see, that it is precisely due to Platonism ("metaphysics" proper) that violence occurs. That is, it is the positing of *the truth*—for Nietzsche "truth" itself is violent—absolutely, as a metanarrative, that leads to kind of fascistic ethic of forced conversion to an ideal. The postmodern argument in general, which Lyotard aptly describes as "incredulity toward metanarratives," largely concedes to this very point, namely that Platonism and its ideal world are the very *cause* of evil and violence.[45] For Girard, I argue, it would be precisely the opposite. Postmodern fails due to the death of God, the death of truth, as a universal that all can share in equally without rivalry or competition. Rather once "God" qua truth dies, all desired objects become finite, for there is nothing supersensible (meta-physical) left to desire. This unbridled desire for the finite, coupled with modern democracy, wherein everyone's desires are now on equal footing and thus equally accessible, will invariably breed immense competition and eventually violence.

The postmodern ethic is in essence a deconstruction of metaphysical originals. It is "good," for postmodernism, in a sense that truth dies, that God dies, since "Truth," or any truth for that matter, is ultimately fascistic. This case at least has been made in postwar Europe in efforts to understand the radical destruction at the hands of the Nazi Party. Hannah Arendt posited an antimetaphysical, anti-Platonic, postmodern reason as a possible answer to the question of *why* such radical evil occurred on such a massive scale in the twentieth century. Her argument (which as we shall see in the next chapter remains essentially the same as Heidegger's) concerns what she calls the "techne model of politics" coupled with the banality of evil.[46] For Arendt, following her teacher Heidegger, radical evil is caused by a political appropriation—misappropriation—of the Greek notion of techne, where the craftsman looks to the ideal Platonic world for the form so as to instantiate it in the material realm.[47] The form completely controls, and the matter wholly submits to be formed by it. In an analogous fashion, then, the ideals of the twentieth century, even if they were harmless *ideally,* inevitably bred violence as they tried to form and fix the world in their own image. One needs only to recall Stalinism and its efforts to instantiate communism to understand Arendt's point. Moreover, Arendt couples her critique of Platonism with that of the banality of evil, namely that all evil is essentially thoughtless and (culpable) ignorance.[48] Evil is not due to the "malice of rage" that lies inherent in being, as Heidegger thinks, but rather to the mediocrity of most people's failure to think, a point no doubt more Socratic.[49] Nevertheless, it is important to highlight Arendt's anti-Platonism as a kind of mouthpiece for the entire postmodern movement and its ethical critique of idealistic Platonism, a critique that we have noted is quite far from Girard and his affirmation of at least a kind of mimetic Platonism qua Christianity.

Girard's tacit consent to a kind of Platonism is highlighted in an essay of his on innovation entitled "Innovation and Repetition."[50] Essentially Girard argues that the concept of innovation drastically changes with the scientific, industrial, and technological revolutions. These revolutions are the result of the constant upsurge of new creativity and genuine innovation. Thus, innovation moves from having an almost wholly negative connotation, due to the philosophical and theological hierarchy and paradigm of essences as the originals, to being an absolute good in modernity. Innovation is directly connected with imitation and has a negative connotation so long as Platonism reigns, that is, so long as there remains an eternal, fixed original as a model. However, as modernity becomes less tolerant of tradition, it sacrifices its originals in favor of the radically novel. Currently, Girard argues, there is an obsession with the novel, to the point that there remains little originality, since everyone is merely copying his or her model negatively. Everyone merely says the opposite of what is perceived to be in vogue. Certainly this is the case, for Girard, in academia, particularly in the humanities, where radical theses are posited simply because they are novel, and not because they necessary provide any insight or explanatory power.[51] Girard sees the uprising and tyranny of the novel as a consequence of the loss of Platonic originals. People are ever more enmeshed in mimetic desire and imitative rivalry, but it remains wholly concealed from them in the name of the fashionable. That is, seeking *not to imitate* has led to absolute imitation, and thus to almost no originality. In seeking to reject imitation altogether, an impossibility for Girard, modernity remains ever more locked into a radical mimesis, the kind of mimesis that is not for the infinite, but for the finite, and thus the kind that leads inevitably to competition and conflict. Ultimately, the modern obsession with imitation, or rather obsession with anti-imitation, is for Girard a kind of blasphemous self-deification, in which humans now seek to be creator ex nihilo, an activity traditionally reserved only for God.

For these reasons, namely the cultural death of Platonism—which, for Nietzsche, is synonymous with "death of God"—and the rapid obsession with innovation, each itself leading to a fierce culture of mimetic rivalry and contagion, Girard considers his thinking *apocalyptic*. However, it is not for these reasons alone. For Girard, with the death of the sacred wrought by the death of Christ comes death to the entire sacrificial system of scapegoating as a method of relieving mimetic tensions. Satan can no longer "cast out Satan." Thus humanity remains in a bind in that it no longer has a surefire way of stopping violence from escalating to catastrophic ends. In other words, for Girard, violence, without the "pressure release" of the scapegoat system, could lead to human beings completely destroying themselves. Thus Girard reads the apocalyptic texts of the New Testament, particular those in the Synoptic Gospels, as indicating the consequences of the rejection of Christ and his Kingdom. For Girard, the "apocalypse" is not something caused by God, but rather the result of human beings being left to their own devices without the ability to dissolve tensions via sacrificial, mob violence (a truth that still remains concealed to many Christians). Christ's teachings therefore became more and more apocalyptic the more Christ realized that humanity would reject him and his message. And yet, if the rejection of Christ leads to an absolute dismantling of the sacrificial system, then human violence could and likely would ultimately escalate exponentially to total destruction.

Thus for Girard human beings are faced with an urgent ultimatum of either embracing nonviolence or perishing.

Given the philosophical implications, Platonic or otherwise, of Girard's mimetic theory, as well as his understanding of the scared, an engagement with the philosophical tradition, particularly postmodernism vis-à-vis Nietzsche and Heidegger, will prove fruitful. Indeed Girard has engaged these two very thinkers explicitly on many occasions. While Girard's critiques of both Nietzsche and Heidegger are quite robust, Girard's admiration for them extends even further. That is, Girard believes both Nietzsche and Heidegger to have come to fundamental and indispensable insights concerning mimetic theory and the sacred, particularly with regard to Nietzsche's understanding of Christianity and the death of God, and Heidegger's understanding of Hellenic metaphysics versus Hebraic thinking. Therefore, it will be necessary to discuss these two philosophers in further detail before indicating points of agreement and disagreement between them and Girard's notion of the sacred and Christianity.

CHAPTER 2

Nietzsche's Religious Hermeneutics

According to Girard, Nietzsche is the most important philosopher *and theologian* of the last hundred years, for Nietzsche understands quite clearly the essence of Christianity better than anyone before. Nietzsche simply despises it. That is, for Girard, Nietzsche understands well that Christianity is a religion of innocent victims, where sacrifice and scapegoating are disregarded in favor of compassion and concern for victims in the spirit of nonviolence. Nietzsche knows that in the biblical texts, victims are always innocent and the collective mob is guilty and that, in myths, the victims are to blame and communities innocent.[1] In other words, Nietzsche sees what no one else could see, namely the absolute uniqueness of Christianity, and thus the fundamental difference between Christianity and all other mythologies and past rituals (including Greek tragedy)—what Nietzsche calls "Dionysian." Nietzsche simply sides with the mythic, the Dionysian, and moreover, attempts to restore mythic thinking to the prominence it once had in antiquity. Furthermore, Nietzsche understands that Christianity is in essence *Platonic*; as Nietzsche famously wrote, "Christianity is Platonism for the people."[2] Thus, Nietzsche, as "Dionysus versus the Crucified," seeks to overturn and overcome metaphysics as Platonism, and in doing so overcome the entire metaphysical backbone to Christianity. As much as Nietzsche's

Dionysian philosophy is antithetical to Christianity, nevertheless, for Girard, Nietzsche remains crucially important precisely because he sees this uniqueness of Christianity and the biblical tradition, and, therefore is not far from Girard's own theory of the sacred. In what follows, I would like to detail the aspects of Nietzsche's "theology" and philosophy as they pertain to my and Girard's concerns with the violent sacred, Christianity, and the overcoming of Platonism. This will involve a brief foray into Nietzsche's *On the Genealogy of Morals* and *The Anti-Christ*, as well as the unpublished notes from his *Nachlass*. However, first it will be necessary to lay out Girard's reflections upon Nietzsche in further detail.

Girard and Nietzsche

Girard discusses Nietzsche in nearly every one of his published works. However, his most concise and pointed philosophical treatment of Nietzsche is in his later work *I See Satan Fall Like Lighting*, in a chapter entitled "The Twofold Nietzschean Heritage."[3] Here Girard begins by discussing the inner logic of National Socialism as an attempt to rid itself of the Judeo-Christian ethic of concern for victims. "The spiritual goal of Hitler's ideology was to root out of Germany, then all of Europe, that calling that Christian tradition places upon all of us: the concern for victims."[4] Girard argues that the Nazis found support for their counter-Christian ethic in the philosophy of Nietzsche (this statement of Girard of course will have to be qualified in what follows). Girard begins by praising Nietzsche as *the* thinker who discovered the "anthropological key" to Christianity, namely, again, the vocation of concern for victims. That is, for Girard, all prior anthropologists and theologians remained too positivistic in their approach to comparative religions, always seeking to level-down Christianity vis-à-vis other religious traditions, showing that Christianity was indeed no different than any other mythical sacrificial tradition. With Nietzsche, however, this was not the case. Nietzsche knew the *facts* of the collective violence of these mythical traditions (for Girard, these all fall under the heading of Nietzsche's "Dionysian") and Christianity to be the same; however the key difference that Nietzsche noticed was not the facts, but the interpretation of the facts, namely the moral interpretation of the meaning of collective violence with regard to the victim. The key passage of Nietzsche's for Girard, a passage he quotes many times in his work, comes from *The Will to Power*, paragraph 1052:

> Dionysus versus the "Crucified": there you have the antithesis. It is *not* a difference in regard to their martyrdom—it is a difference in the meaning of it. Life itself, its eternal fruitfulness and recurrence, creates torment, destruction, the will to annihilation. In the other case, suffering—the "Crucified as the innocent one"—counts as an objection to life, as a formula for condemnation. One will see that the problem is that of the meaning of suffering: whether a Christian meaning or a tragic meaning. In the former case, it is supposed to be the path to a holy existence; in the latter case, being is counted as *holy enough* to justify even a monstrous amount of suffering. The tragic man affirms even the harshest suffering. . . . Dionysus cut to pieces is a *promise* of life: it will be eternally reborn and return again from destruction.[5]

In other words, Dionysus approves of the mob violence and lynching of the victim, in the name of life, vitality, and recurrent cycles of necessary violence as a part of "life" itself; Christianity, however, condemns violence of any kind in the name of the "innocent" one, Jesus. The difference lies not in fact, but in interpretation. Nietzsche likely has in mind here two stories of Dionysus: the story of Dionysus Zagreus, where Dionysus is ripped apart (*sparagmos*) and eaten, and later reborn by Zeus, but also Euripides's *Bacchae*, where Dionysus comes to Thebes in disguise and instigates the *mania* of mob violence toward Pentheus, who is torn apart in a violent rage by the townspeople, led by Pentheus's mother. Dionysus originally is the victim, a martyr even. Nevertheless in all other episodes of the "Dionysian cycle" there is always a *diasparagmos*, a collective lynching and dismembering of a victim instigated by the god himself. The god, both victim and chief murderer, continually instigates "holy lynchings." For Girard, Dionysus is the very god of *mania*, where *mania* is nothing more than "homicidal fury."[6] For Nietzsche, however, it is a matter of the affirmation versus the denial of life vis-à-vis suffering and violence. That is, Christianity amounts to a denial of life, to a denial of these necessary and essential violent elements, whereas Dionysus affirms them, and in doing so affirms violence and thus life itself. Dionysus dismembered is the promise of life, of continual rebirth from destruction and violence. Nietzsche therefore affirms Dionysus *over and against* Jesus, the "Crucified."

Thus Nietzsche's affirmation of Dionysus is tantamount to an affirmation of violence itself, especially violence toward victims of sacrifice as a necessary part of affirming the cyclic nature of life. At the same time, Nietzsche's affirmation of the necessity of Dionysian violence amounts to a justification of human sacrifice for Girard. Girard again cites Nietzsche's *The Will to Power*:

> Through Christianity, the individual was made so important, so absolute, that he could no longer be sacrificed: but the species endures only through human sacrifice . . . Christianity is the counter-principle to the principle of *selection*. If the degenerate and the sick ("the Christian") is to be accorded the same value as the healthy ("the pagan") . . . then unnaturalness becomes law . . . Genuine charity demands sacrifice for the good of the species—it is hard, it is full of self-overcoming, because it needs *human sacrifice*. And this pseudo-humaneness called Christianity wants it established that *no one should be sacrificed*. (WP 246)

Nietzsche here sees the uniqueness of Christianity: it is a concern for victims, for the weak, the sick, and the ill constituted. "Unnaturalness," in the Darwinian sense, "becomes law" in Christianity. Moreover, Nietzsche, like Girard, sees the primary necessity of human sacrifice in the foundation of human culture and society. Thus Nietzsche sees the same insight as Girard: scapegoating is foundational. Nietzsche, however, affirms it, whereas Girard, following Christianity, overturns and abhors it.

It is a matter of perspective. Myth is told from the persecutor's perspective, Christianity from the persecuted's. Indeed, Nietzsche's philosophy, his metaphysics (if Nietzsche could be said to have a "metaphysics") is precisely "perspectivism": "There is *only* a perspective seeing, *only* a perspective 'knowing.'"[7] From the perspective of "Dionysus" (here understood as the mythic writ large) the persecuted are weak, full of resentment and hate toward the healthy and the powerful; from the perspective of the "Crucified," the persecuted are innocent, the scapegoats of the collective mimetic contagion of the angry mob. It is indeed a matter of which perspective one chooses: the mobs' or the victims.' Girard believes Nietzsche sides with the former and thus despises the latter. That Nietzsche sides with the mob, the mythic, is clear, for Girard, due to Nietzsche's famous understanding of *master* versus *slave* morality, wherein the masters represent the active, noble existence that affirms its power in its overflow of life, and the slaves remain reactive, full of resentment against those who are more powerful, more fruitful and success-ful in the game of existence. Affirming, in a way, Nietzsche's perspectivism, it could only be from the *perspective* of the "masters" that one could hold the views Nietzsche holds, namely that Christianity is a religion of the weak and resentful who vie only for the same power and violence that the masters possess.

Slave morality, for Nietzsche, represents the *denial of life*, which is tan-tamount to nihilism par excellence in the form of what Nietzsche dubs *the ascetic ideal*. Characteristic of this ascetic ideal is the unconscious feeling of weakness felt vis-à-vis a more powerful person, a master, and the absolute inability to attain revenge. Therefore this feeling for revenge, for Nietzsche, gets "refelt" again and again in ressentiment.[8] Nietzsche writes, "The slave revolt in morality begins when *ressentiment* itself becomes creative and gives birth to values: the *ressentiment* of natures that are denied the true reaction, that of deeds, and compensate themselves with imaginary revenge" (GM 1:10). In other words, the weak who cannot "win" make necessity a virtue and affirm their own weakness in the form of creating values, for example, compassion, pity, the defense of victims, and so on, around which they can orbit and feel some sense of "power." For Girard this amounts to Nietzsche's ingenious attempt to discredit Judeo-Christian morality, namely by showing that commitment to the concern and defense of innocent victims remains merely hypocritical resentment, of "sympathizing with victims so as to satisfy their resentment of the pagan aristocrats."[9]

Most importantly, Christianity for Nietzsche rejects suffering as neces-sary for life, unlike Dionysianism, which affirms even the harshest suffering as a necessity for life, for continual birth out of violence. In his essay "Nietzsche versus the Crucified," Girard notes that it is most interesting that Nietzsche's criticism against Christianity is *not*, as is the common critique, that of Chris-tianity's "encouraging suffering." Rather, Nietzsche rejects Christianity pre-cisely for its rejection of suffering, for its refusal to see suffering and violence as necessary, and furthermore for its insistence upon the innocence of the victim and therefore the *guilt* of the persecutors. "Nietzsche saw clearly that Jesus died not as a sacrificial victim of the Dionysian type, but against all such sacrifices."[10] In other words, Nietzsche saw that Christianity indicted Dionysus as guilty, and therefore, insofar as Dionysus stands for all primitive mythic, sacrificial systems, Christianity indicted primitive religions and their collective violence as guilty. Indeed, with Christianity, violence itself is put on trial and condemned. Girard writes,

> The Christian Passion is not anti-Jewish as the vulgar anti-Semites believe; it is anti-pagan; it reinterprets religious violence in such a negative fashion as to make its perpetrators feel guilt for committing it, even for silently accepting it. Since all human culture is grounded in this collective violence, the whole human race is declared guilty from the standpoint of the Gospels. Life itself is slandered because life cannot continue and organize itself without this type of violence.[11]

Nietzsche saw this indictment against life and thus rejected Christianity, for violence and human sacrifice are part of the Dionysian cycle of life, and therefore any affirmation of life *must* affirm these very elements. Nietzsche thus says of the Dionysian, "*Dionysus*: sensuality and cruelty. Transitoriness could be interpreted as enjoyment of productive and destructive force, as *continual creation*" (WP 1049). And again,

> The word "*Dionysian*" means: an urge to unity, a reaching out beyond personality, the everyday, society, reality, across the abyss of transitoriness: a passionate-painful overflowing into darker, fuller, more floating states; an ecstatic affirmation of the total character of life as that which remains the same, just as powerful, just as blissful, through all change; the great pantheistic sharing of joy and sorrow that sanctifies and calls good even the most terrible and questionable qualities of life; the eternal will to procreation, to fruitfulness, to recurrence; the feeling of the necessary unity of creation and destruction. (WP 1050)

Each of these pronouncements shows the necessity of the opposites of creation and destruction, joy and sorrow, sensuality and cruelty. Destruction, sorrow, cruelty, violence, and so forth are the very parts of the "whole of life" that, according to Nietzsche, Christianity rejects and pronounces as guilty. Nevertheless, according to Girard, Nietzsche, in his rejection of Christianity as "anti-life," saw the absolute uniqueness of Christianity vis-à-vis all other notions of the sacred. For this reason, Nietzsche, for Girard, remains the most important philosopher and theologian of the last hundred years.

Nietzschean "Morality"

Yet is Girard's reading of Nietzsche fair? Or does Girard simply present Nietzsche as a kind of straw man or foil to further his own ends? We can begin to answer this question by turning to Nietzsche's reflections upon morality in his published writings. Nietzsche's discussion of conscience and guilt in *On the Genealogy of Morals* points to an understanding of human sacrifice and violence consistent with Girard. Here Nietzsche discusses the pleasure and even recreation that primitive humans, before the confines of modern slave conscience, once took in violently punishing. Nietzsche writes,

> *Cruelty* constituted the great festival pleasure of more primitive men and was indeed an ingredient of almost every one of their pleasures: and how naively, how innocently their thirst for cruelty manifested itself, how, as a matter of principle, they posited disinterested malice . . . as a *normal* quality of man. (GM 2:6)

Nietzsche here notes the festival and pleasure primitive humans enjoyed in their practice of violence, indeed as a normal quality of humanity. Moreover Nietzsche notes that from such sadistic pleasure of inflicting violence arose the concept of retributive justice:

> To ask it again: to what extent can suffering balance debts or guilt? To the extent that to *make* suffer was in the highest degree pleasurable, to the extent that the injured party exchanged for the loss he had sustained, including the displeasure caused by the loss, an extraordinary counter-balancing pleasure: that of *making* suffer—a genuine *festival,* something which, as aforesaid, was prized the more highly the more violently it contrasted with the rank and social standing of the creditor. (GM 2:6)

In other words, punishment had a *cathartic* effect on those who felt they were wronged. Inflicting punishment did not "right the wrong" in some abstract, metaphysical sense, but rather enabled the cathartic release of the most primitive of emotions, namely the wanting, needing even, to inflict harm upon one's fellow man so as, so to speak, to balance the debts. Nietzsche, however, takes this one step further and notes a "hard saying," that watching the sufferings of others is in fact *good* for human beings:

> To see others suffer does one good, to make others suffer even more: this is a hard saying but an ancient, mighty, human, all-too-human principle to which even the apes might subscribe; for it has been said that in devising bizarre cruelties they anticipate man and are, as it were, his "prelude." Without cruelty there is no festival: thus the longest and most ancient part of human history teaches—and in punishment there is so much that is *festive*! (GM 2:6)

Nietzsche here seems to again come close to Girard's point about ancient mythology's scapegoat mechanism and its use of sacrifice and violence in order to abate humanity's primitive emotional constitutions. There is indeed, for Nietzsche, something purgative about violence. Cruelty is the *essential* aspect to "festival," or we could say, to religion. This passage amounts to Nietzsche's almost saying flat-out that "violence *is* the sacred."

Nietzsche, in a proto-Freudian manner, later concludes that conscience and guilt are the results of these violent urges no longer having an external outlet and thus needing some form of expression, and hence they were nonetheless directed inwardly. This directing of violence inward, into one's self and toward one's own psyche, is for Nietzsche nothing more than the birth of conscience itself. That is, human beings, addicted to the pleasure of violence and cruelty, must get their "violent fix" somehow, even when such outward violence is no longer societally accepted. Thus they turn inward and inflict harm upon themselves in the form of guilt. This internally directed violence gets hijacked and exponentially exploited in Judeo-Christianity, especially in the later forms of medieval penances, which included not just inward feelings of guilt, but outward expressions of such guilt and contrition that led to practices such as self-flagellation, excessive fasting, and so on. For Nietzsche, had Christianity merely accepted violence's necessity and not condemned it, such practices would have never come to pass. However, as we have seen, Girard likely would explain such exaggerations of violence post-Christianity as symptoms of the removal of the scapegoat mechanism's ability to offer catharsis and the failure by some human beings to forgo violence altogether, as Christ commands.

Now Nietzsche's critique of Christianity extends well beyond that of resentment and the rejection of violence and cruelty. Later in his life, just before his collapse into madness, Nietzsche wrote *The Anti-Christ*, a work largely ignored by most Nietzsche scholars. In this work, Nietzsche's disdain for Christianity's concern for victims becomes the most explicit. Nietzsche also puts forth perhaps his clearest assertions about the will to power. "What is good?—All that heightens the feeling of power, the will to power, power itself in man. What is bad?—All that proceeds from weakness" (A 2). And yet, if that wasn't clear enough, Nietzsche leaves nothing to the imagination as to how this particular dictum applies to Christianity:

> The weak and the ill-constituted should die off [*sollen zu Grunde gehn*]: first principle of *our* philanthropy. And one shall help them to do so. What is more harmful than any vice?—Active sympathy for the ill-constituted and weak—Christianity. (A 2, translation amended)[12]

Christianity is now considered to be the "bad" itself insofar as it proceeds from weakness, insofar as it remains actively sympathetic for the ill-constituted and weak, or we could say, insofar as it has concern for victims. Christianity is for Nietzsche weak precisely due to its obsession with victims and their weakness. Rather Nietzsche argues as a matter of principle that the weak shall perish and that we should even help them to do so. Aside from the obvious inflammatory rhetoric, Nietzsche nevertheless shows us all his cards in his hatred for Christianity's ethic of victims.

It is not just victims, but more so, the *concern* Christianity has for them that Nietzsche criticizes. That is, Christianity, for Nietzsche, remains most obsessed with the virtue of compassion or pity (*Mitleid*). Nietzsche's critique of compassion, however, runs deeper and goes further back than his late manic obsessions with Christianity. That is, Nietzsche's critique of compassion originated as a critique of Schopenhauer (a predecessor and common interlocutor for Nietzsche) and his philosophy concerning the will, the "principle of individuation," and therefore the meaning of suffering in existence. For Schopenhauer, heavily influenced by Buddhism, existence is essentially suffering, due to the "will to life" and its incessant striving, which leads, among other things, to the perception of separateness in existence—the principle of individuation. The will represents an unquenchable desire and necessitates, in a proto-Girardian fashion, antipathy and conflict not only toward other human beings, but toward all of nature as well. The only way "out" of this unbearable suffering of existence is quite simply, for Schopenhauer, compassion. Compassion, *Mit-leid*, literally "suffering with," allows one to pierce the illusion of separateness—what Schopenhauer refers to using an Eastern religious term "the veil of the Maya"—and experience a kind of prerational unity with all of existence. Compassion overcomes difference, separateness itself, and therefore unites human beings to each other; nature no longer appears hostile but "friendly." Nietzsche, quite familiar with Schopenhauer, but disdainful of compassion, reinterprets this overcoming of the principle of individuation in Dionysian terms. In *The Birth of Tragedy*, Apollo represents rationality and the "glorious divine image of the *principium individuationis*," whereas Dionysus represents primordial unity and the blissful overcoming of separateness, the separateness of the ego (*Ich*) itself even.[13] The Dionysian intoxication, in music, dance, festival, and so on, comes to replace the Schopenhauerian compassion as the "cure" to the Apollonian principle of individuation. Moreover, Greek tragedy, the best expression of the Dionysian, leads one to contemplate the beauty of the nauseatingly meaningless nature of existence, in a way that did not *deny life* but rather affirm it in all its vicissitudes, including violence.[14] In other words, for Nietzsche, the Dionysian replaces nihilistic compassion, which denies life, in favor of the Dionysian, which affirms life.

Later, in *The Anti-Christ*, Nietzsche's critique of compassion takes a more Darwinian—even social Darwinian—turn. That is, Nietzsche comes to despise compassion not simply because it "denies life," but because it is weak: "Christianity has taken the side of everything weak, base, ill-constituted, it has made an ideal out of *opposition* to the preservative instincts of strong life" (A 4). Dionysian festival gives the benefits of ecstasy and intoxication, primordial unity, by celebrating all aspects of life, especially strength and vigor, without affirming weakness qua weakness. In one of the most outrageous passages in Nietzsche's entire corpus, Nietzsche equates Christian compassion with depression, and moreover the preserving of that which *ought* to be destroyed:

> Christianity is called the religion of *compassion* [*Mitleid*].—compassion stands in antithesis to the tonic emotions which enhance the energy of the feeling of life: it has a depressive effect. One loses force when one has compassion. The loss of force which life has already sustained through suffering is increased and multiplied even further by compassion. Suffering itself becomes contagious through compassion . . . its morally dangerous character appears in a much clearer light. Compassion on the whole thwarts the law of evolution, which is the law of *selection*. It preserves what is ripe for destruction, it defends life's disinherited and condemned; through the abundance of the ill-constituted of all kinds which it *retains* in life it gives life itself a gloomy and questionable aspect. One has ventured to call compassion a virtue (—in every *noble* morality it counts as weakness—) . . . compassion is *practical* nihilism . . . compassion persuades to *nothingness*! . . . [compassion is] hostile to life. Schopenhauer [therefore] was hostile to life: *therefore* compassion became for him a virtue. (A 7, translation amended)

Distinguishing Nietzscheanism from social Darwinism, at this point, becomes quite difficult. Compassion is depressive, preserving what is "ripe for destruction," and multiplying suffering and making it into a contagion in its nihilistic denial of life, which is synonymous for Nietzsche with a persuasion to "nothingness." Most importantly, Nietzsche links compassion to the defense of the condemned, that is, the victims. Compassion affirms what is weakest and most ill fit for life and vitality and is therefore hostile to life, that is, to Dionysus as the celebration of life in all its circles of birth and decay and violence.

It becomes quite difficult, at this point, to defend Nietzsche's positions. Compassion, concern for victims, is, at least in the twenty-first century, the only *absolute* moral value. No one would dare publicly challenge this virtue's highest standing in our culture. Even those hostile to Christianity likely would not question it. Nevertheless, Nietzsche, for Girard, knew precisely that concern for victims, concern for the innocent, and hostility to violence were the summation of the Gospels. Therefore Nietzsche fought wholeheartedly against these virtues as having any seat at the Dionysian table. Even with the proper "spin," which understands *Mitleid*, not as compassion, but as the worst form of pity, one still has to deal with Nietzsche's hostility toward those who are weak and toward those who are victims.

Nietzsche and Girard are therefore on the same page, so to speak, when it comes to the meaning of Christianity and its virtues. Christianity is concern for the weak; Dionysus despises such weakness in the name of life. For Girard this characterization of "Dionysus versus the Crucified" is indeed quite accurate. It is therefore simply a matter of which *perspective* one chooses: the perspective of myth, of the violent victimizers of the mob, or the perspective of Christianity, of the victimized, of the innocent. It is a matter of choosing, then, between the perspective of Dionysus and the perspective of Jesus. To further the point of Girard and Nietzsche's agreement on the meaning of Christianity vis-à-vis victimization and violence, Nietzsche, alongside Girard, argues that the very idea that the Christian God would require sacrifice—the guilt sacrifice of his Son—is absurd, and mere "paganism":

> God gave his Son for the forgiveness of sins, as a *sacrifice*. All at once it was all over with the Gospel! The *guilt sacrifice*, and that in its most repulsive, barbaric form, the sacrifice of the *innocent man* for the sins of the guilty! What atrocious paganism! (A 41)

Here Nietzsche's insights are twofold. First, Nietzsche recognizes the pagan nature of the God requiring a sacrifice to atone for sins. The idea that God would need blood is a pagan, Dionysian, characteristic. Furthermore, Nietzsche again recognizes that Jesus is innocent. Again, we could say that Nietzsche penetrates to the heart of the uniqueness of Christianity in his denial of the substitutionary atonement model, the very model Girard himself thought to be pagan.[15] Nietzsche understands, rather, that violence is an entirely human characteristic, one that is essential to human beings and to human culture.

Nietzsche's main critique of Christianity has therefore a recurrent pattern that is perhaps best expressed in his understanding of the Christian conception of God vis-à-vis the pagan. For Nietzsche a Dionysian god must embrace the whole of life, on both extremes of pleasure and pain, good and bad. Such a god, Nietzsche notes, "must be able to be both useful and harmful, both friend and foe—he is admired in good and bad alike" (A 16). Nietzsche's conception of the pagan god(s) is precisely in line with Girard's, as the mythic god, for Girard, is both good and evil: evil, as the guilty victim deserving of the collective lynching, and yet good, as the resurrected deity to whom the reconciled community ritually sacrifices. The Christian God represents, therefore, according to Nietzsche, the "*anti-natural* castration of a God into a God of the merely good" (A 16). That is, Nietzsche rightly understands that the Christian God is wholly good, in no way evil, and most importantly nonviolent. What amounts to a castration of God for Nietzsche is for Girard the height of the beauty of Christian revelation. The innocent God suffering the collective violence of the guilty mob reveals, for Girard, the infinite love of God for humanity and simultaneously God's condemnation of violence. This weakness of the God in suffering coupled with the guilt of the condemnation of violence amounts, for Nietzsche, to the nihilism of Christianity. Again, according to Girard, Nietzsche and Christianity agree as to the facts, and even upon the interpretation of those facts. They merely disagree on the better perspective.

Finally, Nietzsche's *Anti-Christ* understands remarkably and clearly the essence of Jesus's teaching as teaching about a life of love and nonviolence. Nietzsche likens the personality of Jesus to that of "the Idiot" of Dostoyevsky's novel (A 29). For Nietzsche, Jesus is joyous and overflowing with life and goodness, but is wholly misunderstood by the world, especially his followers. Nietzsche argues that the "profoundest saying of the Gospels," in a sense their summary and essence, is simply "resist not evil" (A 29). Nietzsche speaks with admiration of the historical Jesus, one whom he considered to be free of resentment and full of love. Although Girard does not comment on this aspect of Nietzsche's understanding of Jesus, as noted earlier, Girard certainly would be in agreement with Nietzsche's distilling all of Christ's teachings down to the love of enemies and the nonresistance to violence.

Nietzsche thus writes that there was only one real Christian, "and he died on the Cross" (A 39). That is, Nietzsche draws a stark contrast between the historical figure of Jesus, and Christianity—particularly *Pauline* Christianity—that came afterward. The latter, Nietzsche argues, distorts the former in the spirit of resentment. Apparently for Nietzsche, perhaps inconsistently, Jesus seems to occupy some middle position outside of the dialectical counterpositions of "Christianity" and "Dionysus." Jesus, the historical Jesus at least, seems then to be something other than "The Crucified," at least insofar as Jesus is "superior to all resentment," unlike Christianity, which is Platonism for the masses that runs off of the fuel of resentment (A 39). Yet it would be difficult for Nietzsche simply to situate the historical Jesus in the mythic, Dionysian camp, given Nietzsche's own concession that Jesus was in fact wholly opposed to all violence and cruelty (A 39). Thus Nietzsche's musings on the figure of Jesus are quite curious given not only that these musings arise in his text *The Anti-Christ*, but also that Jesus does not seem to fit neatly into any of Nietzsche's intellectual categories concerning the will to power. However, we can say for certain that for Nietzsche Jesus does not embody the spirit of resentment that Nietzsche thinks so plagued Jesus's followers. Nietzsche seeks to liberate Jesus from the interpretation of his crucifixion by his followers, namely the collective guilt for persecuting the innocent. Thus, Nietzsche seeks to liberate Jesus from the *Christian* indictment against life, whereas Girard thinks these two are one and the same.

It is worth noting that for Girard, Nietzsche misunderstands his own conception of ressentiment vis-à-vis will to power, and thus misunderstands will to power itself. Recall the distinction between the accuser (Satan) of the mythic mob and the Paraclete (the Holy Spirit) of the innocent victim. Girard believes that resentment actually resides on the side of the mob and not on the side of the weak victim. Girard inverts, therefore, Nietzsche's perspective concerning masters and slaves. Resentment, for Girard, is a mere form of mimetic desire, and thus will to power plays by the same rules, so to speak, as mimetic desire, which, if not checked, leads to rivalry and violence. In other words, to think will to power apart from mimesis, as Nietzsche did, is an absolute impossibility for Girard. Will to power is, by nature, competitive, and if competitive then rivalrous, and if rivalrous then violent, and if violent then ultimately resentful. Girard ultimately sees no difference between violence and resentment. Furthermore, even Nietzsche's seeming solution to resentment in the Übermensch or the noble morality, as the morality of victory and success, proves to be no more than the unbridled "search for the insurmountable obstacle," the ultimate *diabolos*, as the ultimate challenge to overcome.[16] Thus the will to power is nothing more than the *ideology* of mimetic desire, which furthers mimetic desire's own ends without being aware of them.[17] In other words, will to power writ large, and even in the noble morality, remains *eo ipso* competitive and thus fated to violence—even if it is the violence of momentary revenge, and not that of lasting ressentiment, which it almost always is not. That is, insofar as the supreme expression of will to power is the endless overcoming of obstacles, then, for Girard, this amounts to nothing other than the "supreme expression" of mimetic rivalry, which always arises when the model becomes the obstacle. If this is so, then Nietzsche's will to power is simply *violence* itself in disguise as nobility.

Will to Power as Violence

The idea that Nietzschean will to power is synonymous with violence requires some unpacking. It is not a claim made by Girard, as his analyses are often limited more to the anthropological than the philosophical, by his own admission. Nevertheless there is an astounding metaphysical claim that can be unearthed from Girard's analysis of Nietzsche, namely will to power *is* violence, and violence *is* will to power. Heidegger's analysis of Nietzsche here proves helpful. The most remarkable aspect of Heidegger's reading of Nietzsche is that Heidegger understands Nietzsche as, strangely enough, primarily a metaphysician, a metaphysician obsessed with *overcoming metaphysics*. Even though Nietzsche's fundamental aim is to overcome metaphysics, Heidegger nevertheless understands Nietzsche's will to power, along with his Eternal Return, as the essential elements that constitute Nietzsche's ontology. That is, for Heidegger, Nietzsche's "basic metaphysical position" concerns the reconciliation of the will to power and the eternal return into a singular thought, namely the overcoming of metaphysics, and thus the overcoming of "being" with "becoming," such that the will to power *and* the Eternal Return *name* being as becoming. Heidegger's task is therefore to sublate, in a Hegelian manner, these two concepts into one. It is by way of this Hegelian sublation of will to power and Eternal Return into becoming that the violence of Nietzsche's philosophy becomes apparent.

Essentially Heidegger argues that the will to power and eternal return correspond to the basic metaphysical categories of essence and existence, such that will to power names *what* beings essentially *are*, whereas Eternal Return names *how* beings *are*.[18] In other words, beings, things, as will to power occur eternally again and again. Beings are essentially will to power, in that they are constantly striving toward greater and greater power, that is, greater challenges and *obstacles* to overcome, so as to increase their feeling of power. "What is happiness?—the feeling that power *increases*—that a resistance is overcome" (A 2). The key quotation as to the essence of will to power, for Heidegger, lies in a passage from *The Will to Power*:

> The standpoint of 'value' is the standpoint of conditions of preservation and enhancement for complex forms of relative life-duration within the flux of becoming. (WP 715)

Will to power operates fundamentally by positing and stabilizing reality in the form of "values" so as to promote "life." In a Darwinian fashion, will to power schematizes reality, stabilizes it, forms it even, in terms of the *creation* of values, and seeks to overcome and *destroy* these values qua self-challenges in order to experience a heightened sense of life. Will to power posits values, and such values are posited solely *so as* to be overcome. These values are challenges, resistances, to be overcome for the preservation and enhancement of life itself. In short, will to power *stabilizes* becoming into being in order to increase its sense of power. This stabilizing of chaos into stability, of becoming into being, reveals the essence of will to power as nothing more than wanting more and more power. Will to power challenges itself toward ever more power by positing values as resistances in order to overcome them. Heidegger notes that "power is only power only if and as long as it is enhancement of power."[19] Will to power, then, *creates so as to destroy*, thereby increasing its power. Moreover, there remains no telos to will to power's drive toward enhancement; the only telos is simply more power. "Values" are posited *in order to* be overcome. This is the activity of will to power itself. Will to power is the movement through ossification and petrification of reality to its destruction and deconstruction so as to feel power. Yet, according to Heidegger, if the will to power is nothing more than the stabilizing and destabilizing of becoming in an endless striving for more power, then will to power itself is revealed to be nothing more than becoming itself, for becoming is the very process of the ossification and destruction of sundry stages of power, toward no goal, ad infinitum. That is, since will to power's creation and destruction of value does nothing more than stabilize and destabilize reality, will to power remains identical to the process of ossification/deossification of becoming itself. Thus will to power in its very definition leads to the passing from will to power over into becoming, conceptually and actually. To think the essence of will to power, as the essence of beings, is to inevitably think becoming itself in its very essence. Heidegger writes,

> For Nietzsche, the pallid term *Becoming* is replete with a content that proves to be the essence of will to power. Will to power is the overpowering of power. *Becoming* does not mean the indefinite flux of an amorphous alternation of fortuitously occurring states. But neither does *Becoming* mean "development" toward a goal. Becoming is the power advancement through sundry stages of power. In Nietzsche's language, *Becoming* means animation—holding sway on its own terms—of will to power as the fundamental trait of beings. Hence all Being is "Becoming."[20]

In other words, becoming is change, but "organized" change and thus not mere chaos. Becoming is organized in such a way as to be without a goal or purpose, akin to imagining Aristotelian change, as the reduction from potency to act guided and caused by its telos as its teleological cause, yet precisely *without* the guidance of any telos. Rather, becoming is merely the advancement of power as the sole causal motivation. Becoming is then the process of *overpowering power* and, as such, is the will to power itself. Both becoming and will to power name the process of the overpowering of power. Therefore, dialectically, thinking the will to power through to its essence necessarily leads to thinking becoming's essence. They are the same thought, for they name the same reality.

Yet for Heidegger in the will to power's passing over into becoming we find that it has actually disclosed itself as the Eternal Return of the Same. Thus, in Hegelian terms, the Eternal Return appears to be the "truth" of the will to power. Heidegger presents this point quite succinctly:

> Every being, insofar as it *is*, and is *as* it is, is 'will to power.' . . . But power is power only as enhancement of power. To that extent that it is truly power, alone determining all beings, power does not recognize the worth or value of anything outside of itself. [Will to power] . . . tolerates no end outside of beings as a whole. Now, because all being as will to power—that is, as incessant self-overpowering—must be a *continual "becoming,"* and because such "becoming" cannot move "toward an end" *outside* its own "farther

and farther," but is ceaselessly caught up in the cyclical increase of power to which it reverts, then being as a whole too, as this power-conforming becoming, must itself always recur again and bring back the same.[21]

Will to power as becoming then *eternally becomes* again and again. The process of will to power's search for power is endless, as it continues to ossify and self-destruct as becoming, and it does this endlessly, eternally. Beings essentially are will to power and occur eternally. In other words, will to power endlessly surmounts obstacles, and this endless surmounting is the very process of becoming itself.

Recall that for Nietzsche, both creation and destruction, which includes violence and cruelty, are essential to embracing the whole of the Dionysian perspective on existence that would affirm life. Dionysus's death and destruction—exemplified in the myth of his dismembering—are just as essential as his continual rebirth. Any affirmation of life must affirm, rather than excise, violence and cruelty. "Life itself, its eternal fruitfulness and recurrence, creates torment, destruction, the will to annihilation. . . . Dionysus cut to pieces is a *promise* of life: it eternally reborn and return from destruction" (WP 1052). Will to power, as becoming, and as eternally reoccurring, represents, in metaphysical terms, Nietzsche's affirmation of the endless cyclical violence of primitive mythology. Life itself, for Nietzsche, is this very process of mythic violence, and, when thought metaphysically, it is none other than the will to power's eternally becoming. Such metaphysics concerning the necessity of destruction in the endless process of becoming grounds quite nicely Nietzsche's affirmation of the necessity of sacrifice, violence, and cruelty as essential to human existence. Mythic violence rests on metaphysical violence. *Will to power is violence itself.*

Girard expressly links the will to power and the Eternal Return with the violence belonging wholly to paganism.[22] Furthermore, Nietzsche's metaphysics of will to power's endlessly becoming grounds the inner logic of mythic, cyclical violence that results in scapegoating. Nietzsche's genius lies in the fact that, in his thought, the idea of violence being part of the endless eternal cycle of existence (becoming) becomes completely transparent, so much so that he could put forth an ontology based upon this mythic cycle. Nietzsche's metaphysics of will to power and the Eternal Return are then wholly Dionysian and explicitly so. For the first time, then, with Nietzsche, myth becomes self-aware of its own brutality and violence *and* its endless cyclical nature, and yet nevertheless affirms itself. For this reason, Girard argues that Nietzsche's sole task is that of the resurrection of myth. Nietzsche understood clearly that Christianity, in a sense, had destroyed myth by exposing it for what it truly was, namely the mob violence against the weak and innocent; Nietzsche however, in his Dionysius against the Crucified, seeks to resurrect and restore myth to its original place, and in so doing to restore mythic violence, even the mythic violence of human sacrifice.

That Nietzsche saw so clearly into Christianity's essence, while also rejecting it, is for Girard simultaneously Nietzsche's genius and madness. Thus Girard writes that "Nietzsche's only error, a properly *Luciferian* error (in the sense of 'bringer of light'), was to have chosen violence against the innocent truth of the victim, a truth that Nietzsche himself was the only one to glimpse."[23] Nietzsche's descent into madness results from his choice of perspective, his siding with Dionysian *mania* against the weakness of victims, whom he regarded as inferior. For Girard, Nietzsche paid for this choice with his life.[24]

Nietzsche's Critique of Metaphysics

Yet the affirmation of Dionysian violence against "the Crucified" presents only one side of Nietzsche's project of "overcoming metaphysics." For Nietzsche, as well as later for Heidegger, metaphysics is quite simply Platonism; Platonism *is* metaphysics.[25] These terms are one and the same, at least for both Nietzsche and Heidegger. Now since metaphysics is Platonism, and Christianity is essentially watered-down Platonism, the heart of Nietzsche's metaphysical attack against Christianity aims at its Platonic core, namely the theory of the dual, split world.[26] Platonism's splitting of reality into the apparent and true world is nothing other than a split between becoming and being, with being given the place of privilege as the "true" over and against that which becomes. Yet Nietzsche finds at the heart of this split world an even more potent form of ressentiment than that discussed earlier vis-à-vis Christianity as slave morality. In his *Thus Spoke Zarathustra*, Nietzsche provides a somewhat deeper insight into the meaning of revenge and resentment. "This, yes, this alone is revenge itself: the will's repugnance against time and its 'it was.'"[27] Revenge hates time, in particular, revenge hates, revolts against, time's passing, time's "it was." In short, revenge revolts against *becoming*, for it cannot stand becoming's lack of permanency. This "metaphysical *ressentiment*" goes a step deeper than mere resentment against the noble and powerful and resents the heart of reality itself: becoming. Metaphysical revenge revolts against reality itself, insofar as reality "is" not permanent, but is becoming, that is, insofar as it lacks the constitution of "being," of "isness," of staticness. Platonic metaphysics, then, in positing the split world, the world of being over becoming, is really driven by ressentiment, a revenge against reality that creates, out of this revenge, the other "true" world. Thus "the *ressentiment* of metaphysicians against actuality is here creative," in that it creates the other world, and even the very concept of God itself (WP 579). God is nothing more than a mythical stand-in for the true world of being. Indeed, the God of metaphysics is precisely being itself as the *ens causa sui* or the *ens realissimum*, that is, the self-caused being or the most real being. God is moreover he who metes out "justice" (another form of revenge) for the oppressed, and grants a life beyond temporality in eternity. Therefore, being, truth, and God are one and the same for Nietzsche, not only conceptually, but also in origin, insofar as they all arise out of the spirit of revenge, revenge against time, becoming, and reality itself.

Revenge therefore, for Nietzsche is the core of metaphysics as *meta-ta-phusika*, that which goes "beyond the physical" to the meta-physical. Moreover, revenge lies at the heart of metaphysics as *theology*.[28] It is revenge that is repulsed by becoming's impermanence and thus seeks to stabilize such permanence in being, in the true world. Thus Nietzsche's inversion of Platonism as the positing of the world of becoming over that of being is an endeavor aimed at essentially "overcoming revenge." According to Heidegger, the overcoming of revenge marks the one essential thought that Nietzsche spent his lifetime trying to properly think; it is Nietzsche's "true one and only thought, which he thought even if he did not announce on every occasion or always in the same way."[29] For Heidegger this thought is best glimpsed in a passage from *Zarathustra*: "*For that man be released from revenge*: this is for me the bridge to the highest hope, and a rainbow after long storms."[30] If revenge, ressentiment, against time and becoming is the very source of metaphysics, then to overcome such revenge would be at the same time to overcome metaphysics. Such overcoming of metaphysics represents then an all-out assault on "being" for Heidegger. Therefore, for Nietzsche, to overcome revenge, being must be replaced (and overcome) with becoming. This replacement is ipso facto the overcoming of revenge, for it is revenge that enables the *meta* in metaphysics.[31] That is to say, revenge motivates the transcendence from the physical, sensible world of becoming to the metaphysical, supersensible world of being. So then, to overcome revenge is to overcome being, and vice-versa.

Thus there are positive, even beautiful, elements to Nietzsche's thinking, and the overcoming of resentment and revenge is certainly one of them. However, given Nietzsche's scathing critique of compassion and of concern for victims, it would be foolish to assume that this overcoming of revenge is compatible with other humanistic values such as these. The Dionysian world affirms both good and evil, and that evil includes violence.

It is worth noting that Nietzsche's solution as to *how* to overcome this Platonically divided world occurs precisely in his metaphysic of the Eternal Return, where the totality of "what is" is named as complete becoming, thus inverting the Platonic schema of being and becoming entirely and destroying being in favor of endless becoming. Being becomes a mere "vapor." Being is a mere temporary phenomenon grounded in the transitory ossification of becoming wrought by the will to power. Being has no ontological status of its own, but rather takes its "life" from the will to power's own becoming. This stripping of any ontological status from being marks the essence of Nietzsche's overturning of Platonism, for being has now been made becoming; "what is" is now "what becomes," that is, will to power. Nietzsche therefore writes in sum,

> This my Dionysian world of the eternally self-creating, the eternally self-destroying, this mystery world of the twofold voluptuous delight, my "beyond good and evil," without goal, unless the joy of the circle is itself a goal without will, unless a ring feels good will toward itself—do you want a *name* for this world? A *solution* for all its riddles? A *light* for you, too, you best-concealed, strongest, most intrepid, most midnightly men?—*This world is the will to power—and nothing besides!* And you yourselves are also this will to power—and nothing besides. (WP 1067)

The world then *is* will to power, and nothing besides. That is, the world is ceaseless and cyclical becoming that contains no true, transcendent world, but rather merely an infinite play of various arrangements of power.

In Nietzsche, there is no transcendent world of patterns to imitate as in Platonism. Rather than imitate the transcendent, for Nietzsche one must become an artist, for it is art that creates values insofar as it *consciously* stabilizes becoming into being, and thus into a challenge or "obstacle" to be overcome. Indeed art is the very activity of the will to power's value creation and destruction, and thus of the will to power's own self-overcoming. Thus art *mimics* or imitates the Dionysian world in its continual creativity and destruction. Yet Dionysian imitation is really nothing of the kind, insofar as there remains no "original" to imitate or copy. Rather the Dionysian artist creates originally from out of the storehouse of the will to power itself. It is a kind of mimesis without an original to imitate, and thus simply mimes the original activity of the will to power, namely its cyclical creativity and destruction.

Art then is the very process of will to power's forming of becoming into being, into a value that self-challenges *so as* to be overcome. Yet, insofar as art remains a kind of mimesis without original, it is itself the original in its very activity. Nietzsche often contrasts art with truth, where truth remains a degraded form of art, a kind of forgotten lie. That is, art is will to power's original forming of becoming into value, whereas truth mistakes the original lie of art for something that actually "is." In other words, truth relates to reality as *already formed* by the will to power, and mistakes this merely petrified becoming as being, and therefore relates to it as "what is," as what is "true." Since for Nietzsche, "there is no truth" (WP 540), rather only the artist's—the will to power's—myriad of lies, the Platonist mistakes these lies for reality, whereas the artist—the Dionysian—remains conscious of these lies. Thus art is a lie—a lie that "becoming *is*"—but a conscious one, whereas truth remains merely a lie, a forgotten, unconscious lie. The Platonist then, in believing that a value "is," believes he can imitate this lie. Nietzsche's overturning of Platonism then amounts to an *overturning of mimesis* itself, and thus an overturning of the relationship between art and truth. Art takes precedence over truth, for truth remains a mere fiction of the creative reactivity of resentment, a belief that a mimesis of the transcendent is possible. Art, however, recognizes that there is neither the transcendent nor "being," but rather only becoming and only the ossified created forms of becoming that have been formed by the will to power. Thus Nietzsche writes that "we have art so as not to perish from the truth" (WP 822), for art is "worth more than the truth" (WP 853).

Nietzsche's overcoming of Platonism then in essence is a reinterpretation of mimesis, where mimesis imitates only itself, and not some pregiven original. Mimesis for Nietzsche is no mere copy of the transcendent, but rather the very activity of the will to power's value positing, which mimes the reality of endless, cyclical becoming itself. This endless cycle is the Dionysian world of creative and destructive violence, the positing of obstacles so as to be overcome. This self-referential mimesis of the will to power is then indeed *a mimesis of violence*, for the will to power *is* violence. For Girard, as we saw, this positing of surmountable obstacles eventually leads to the search for the insurmountable obstacle, the ultimate *skandalon*, and thus will always end in mimetic frenzy and violence. That is, once the transcendent world of truth and being is abolished, there remains nothing left to imitate but the desires of others, for it is an illusion to think that there is something such as "existential authenticity," where one would be completely original.[32] "Authenticity" in the Nietzschean or Heideggerian sense remains for Girard pure fantasy. It is a dream to imagine that one imitates only oneself and only one's will to power. In reality, such thinking entrenches one all the more in mimetic rivalry and violence. Modern individualism, of which existential authenticity remains merely a symptom, amounts to a desperate denial of the fact of mimetic desire. For Girard, the "who" of Dasein in its "everydayness," the inauthentic, "they" self (*das Man*) of Heidegger's *Sein und Zeit*, is in reality the more accurate description of the human being, insofar as human beings indeed borrow desires from others and can never conjure "authentic" desires from the depths of their being.[33] Thus Nietzsche's desire for complete originality, in, for example, the Übermen*sch*, remains for Girard an absolute impossibility, and leads Nietzsche to formulate an ideology of mimetic desire, and thus a metaphysics of violence in the will to power.

For Girard, Nietzsche's overcoming of Platonism not only fails, but leads to the most violent ideology possible, a metaphysics of violence of which Nietzsche himself was well aware and indeed affirmed, but under the guises of authenticity and self-mastery. Nietzsche's mind could not hold out against his own metaphysics and led, as it ought to have, to Dionysian madness. Nietzsche's alignment with the perspective of the persecutors, the Dionysian mob of violent frenzy, leads to an affirmation of violence and a failure to see its injustice; moreover, it leads to a rabid disgust for compassion, as well for the "weak and ill constituted." Nietzsche's "Dionysus versus the Crucified" is in reality Dionysus versus "innocent victims," and thus, for Girard, is the only philosophy that is able to give voice to and make sense of Nazism. Even if Nazism's appropriation of Nietzsche is not what Nietzsche would have intended—for Nietzsche despised anti-Semitism as much as he despised compassion—nevertheless, for Girard, Nietzscheanism is the only philosophy capable of clarifying the logic of Nazism, and is thus, in a way, the inner essence of the movement.[34] Indeed, Girard faults Heidegger for effectively defanging this connection between Nazism and Nietzsche, insofar as Heidegger's reading seeks to remove the religious element in favor of the metaphysical.[35] As I will argue in the next chapter, Girard's reading here is mostly accurate. However, it fails to see the real question at stake for Heidegger, namely the question of the priority of metaphysics over ethics— a priority Levinas later would contest. Regardless, Girard's sobering claims concerning Nietzsche's connection to the logic of Nazism stand insofar as both are united by a logic of self-mastery, an affirmation of violence, and a disgust for victims—in other words, an *anti-Christianity*.

For Girard, given that the fascism of Hitlerism so miserably failed, it is no longer possible to condemn innocent victims. Indeed despite the radical relativism of postmodernity, the concern for victims remains axiomatic and the seemingly sole absolute value. However, Nazism's anti-Christian attitude remains, and thus what resulted from postwar Europe and America is a new kind of fascism that affirms violence, yet only *in the name of victims*. That is, it is only possible to persecute now if one persecutes the perceived "persecutors of the innocent." Thus mob lynches continue, yet under the guise of "justice" for victims, for minorities, for the poor, for the weak, and so on. This for Girard constitutes the rise of "victim power."[36] Girard seems to suggest that Nietzsche's anxiety about victims' resentment is actually fulfilled in this postmodern ethic, in that the defense of victims is used as the excuse to persecute, to *accuse*, the perceived persecutors. Even if the persecutors are actually guilty, Girard thinks that this persecution amounts to a reconfiguration of mythic violence insofar as the scapegoating mechanism is resurrected; again despite the scapegoats' actual guilt. I take Girard to mean that it is never acceptable, in the end, to persecute, to accuse, and thus to scapegoat, again, *even if* the persecutors are guilty—a point that Girard does not readily concede. Now, this does not mean that Girard is simply affirming persecutors, but rather Girard is disavowing violence in any form, including the "just violence" of the defense of victims. For such just violence merely imitates the injustice it seems to combat, and thus becomes entangled in the very game it seeks to end.

The insights we can draw from here are twofold: for one, postmodernity is not as nihilistic and relativist as it thinks itself to be. It axiomatically accepts the *Judeo-Christian* principle of concern for victims, and thus remains still deeply rooted in Judeo-Christianity. Nietzsche of course knew this and thus sought to completely eradicate this concern, and Christianity along with it. Second, for Girard, we are living through a "caricatural 'Ultra-Christianity' that tries to escape from the Judeo-Christian orbit by 'radicalizing' the concern for victims in an anti-Christian manner."[37] Girard then does agree with Nietzsche in that there is a kind of resentment-fueled "Christianity" in postmodernity, as it remains possible to persecute in the name of Christianity, in a bastardized and parodic manner: persecution in the name of victims. In this parody, the violence and hatred of the mob remains, except now it is directed at the perceived "mob" or the perceived lynchers of the innocent. If Christianity represents the nonviolent defense of victims, it is only the satanic parody—the Antichrist—that is the violent defense of victims. It still uses violence to control violence. Christianity only works, for Girard, if it is nonviolent, for nonviolence imitates Christ and Christ's Passion. However, if one seeks to follow Christ, one inevitably will be forced into a situation like that of Peter, namely a situation in which one must choose to persecute or to be persecuted.

CHAPTER 3

Heidegger's Violent Sacred

Girard's reading of Heidegger, like his reading of Nietzsche, focuses on Heidegger as a *religious* thinker, specifically, a thinker of the violent sacred. Heidegger, like Nietzsche, glimpses an essential insight about Christianity, even though Heidegger himself winds up on the opposite side of this insight. In particular, Heidegger gleans *the* fundamental distinction between the Greek Logos and the Hebraic Logos, arguing that each is sui generis, distinct from the other. Girard agrees with this insightful distinction, but disagrees with Heidegger's interpretation and meaning of it. For Girard, the Greek Logos remains inextricably bound with the violent sacred, whereas the Hebraic Logos amounts to a twisting-free of this violence in favor of the nonviolent holy, which reaches its culmination in Christianity in the incarnate Logos that is violently rejected by the world. Thus for Girard, the movement from the Greek Logos to the Christian Logos constitutes a positive progression in the history of philosophy, whereas for Heidegger this movement names the "withdrawal" and "forgetting" of being, a regression whereby being and the sacred become concealed. Girard's contentions with Heidegger extend ultimately, then, to the question of the interpretation of the history of metaphysics and its entanglement with Christianity, and whether this entangling is progressive or regressive. It is a question, then, of how to evaluate the entire history of philosophical thinking, especially with regard to the question of the sacred. Is metaphysics a positive or negative movement in thinking? Is ontotheology ultimately an advance in conceiving of the holy, or the holy's complete eclipse? In what follows, I will argue with Girard against Heidegger's criticisms of the history of Greek metaphysics, in particular his favoring of the Greek over the Hebraic Logos, as well as his critique of metaphysics as ontotheology. This involves explicating in detail Heidegger's understanding of the history of being in Western metaphysics, which includes a discussion of Heidegger's own critique of Nietzsche, something which Girard and Girard scholarship largely ignores. But the question I seek to answer in this chapter is ultimately whether or not Girard's reading of Heidegger, as a thinker of the violent sacred, is correct. If the answer to this question is yes, then a case can finally be made in favor of ontotheology over and against Heidegger's critical reading of metaphysics and his understanding of God that ensues.

Terminology and Context

Before beginning any discussion of Heidegger, it is essential to come to a basic understanding of his fundamental terminology, as well as his overall project. A common criticism of Heidegger is that his terminology is largely unintelligible, for he uses terms like "being" and "truth" in a variety of ways and contexts. Thus a general consensus of approximation as to what these terms mean will be necessary before discussing Heidegger's more particular thoughts on the history of philosophy. Such a consensus will help us to better understand his overall project of overcoming metaphysics.

Heidegger, like Nietzsche, is concerned primarily with the "overcoming of metaphysics" by way of a suspicious hermeneutic, where metaphysics' unthought grounds, or conditions for possibility, are to be unearthed. For Nietzsche, this unthought ground is simply will to power; for Heidegger, it is being (*das Sein, das Seyn*). Only when this ground of metaphysics is fully revealed can an unraveling of metaphysics take place, and thus can a rethinking of the meaning of being and of the meaning of the holy occur. Heidegger's *Seinsfrage*, then, is an entirely new question, a nonmetaphysical question, insofar as any inquiry into metaphysics' conditions already asks a question outside of the realm of metaphysics. In a sense, then in simply posing the *Seinsfrage*, Heidegger's project of overcoming metaphysics has already commenced.

Throughout the history of metaphysics, beginning with Plato and ending with Nietzsche's absolute inversion of Plato, "being" is conceived under the domain of a certain question, namely the question of *what*. What is being? What is being's meaning? The only answer that can be given therefore is one of *whatness* (quiddity) or *essence*. The question is thus already limited before it is even posed, for metaphysics inquires into the being of beings as to their whatness and essence, or, as Heidegger often calls it, their beingness (*Seiendheit*). Heidegger, therefore, in seeking the conditions for possibility of this question as *the* question of metaphysics, seeks to change the question from *what* to *how*. That is, *how* does being happen? Or, how does being occur in such a way so as to enable metaphysics and metaphysical inquiry itself? For Heidegger, this question of the *how* has been concealed or forgotten as the "forgetting of being" itself (*Vergessenheit des Seins*) in that the question of *what* has continually crowded out this question.

In another sense, the question of *what* is also the question of *why*. That is, "Why is a being in fact a being?" or, What is a being's *cause* or *ground* (*der Grund*)? What is the *reason* (*der Grund*) behind beings? Thus for Heidegger, metaphysics' deepest question is, "Why are there beings and not just nothing?" The *Seinsfrage* then, as an inquiry into metaphysics' conditions, asks how it is even possible to ask this question. "Why the why?" or rather, how can the why—even the ultimate question as to why—be put forth? This involves however first understanding what metaphysics itself essentially *is*. Thus the question "What is metaphysics?" if posed in the right manner, is simultaneously the *Seinsfrage*, insofar as both questions really are asking about the conditions for the possibility of metaphysical thinking. For example, in Heidegger's famous lecture "What Is Metaphysics?" (1929), he initially poses the question in terms of *what*—what is metaphysics?—but shows that to genuinely ask this question is no longer to ask it in terms of what, but rather in terms of *how*, namely, how does metaphysics get under way?

What then is metaphysics? Metaphysics, as *meta ta phusika* ("beyond the physical"), names the philosophical discipline that passes beyond beings to their beingness (again, synonymous with essence, whatness, cause, etc.), and thus, according to Aristotle, studies being qua being, or beings insofar as they are intelligible. This study requires *transcending* beings, that is, transcending the fact *that* beings are to *what* being essentially *are.* Metaphysics "splits the world in two" by posing the question as to the what or why of beings and therefore seeks to transcend a being to its beingness. Heidegger's inquiry into metaphysics' conditions is then an inquiry into *transcendence* itself, and, as such, is no longer metaphysics, but *meta*-metaphysics, insofar as it asks how asking why is even possible.

Since this question of the how of the why cannot be asked metaphysically—even if it ostensibly begins with a question as to "what"—Heidegger's approach to this question is deconstructive, and thus phenomenological. That is, in asking, "What is metaphysics?" Heidegger allows for the conditions behind this question to disclose themselves. Such disclosure is simultaneously both deconstructive and phenomenological, since in seeking metaphysics' "ground" metaphysics itself begins to unravel, and in its unraveling reveals what lies "behind" it. Thus Heidegger's "phenomenological method" is nothing more than, by way of deconstruction, an allowing for a disclosure of a being's "truth," where truth is understood in the original Greek sense, according to Heidegger, as *a-letheia,* or unconcealment. Quite simply, then, Heidegger's phenomenological method is to allow for something to disclose itself in its truth. Yet how does the disclosure of metaphysics (and thus the conditions for metaphysics) occur? How can the *how* of the *why* show itself? That is, what makes possible the *distinction,* in the split world, between the apparent world and the true world, between a being and its beingness? How does one, in a Platonic sense, "advance up the line" to the intelligible world?

Nietzsche of course understood the answer to these questions to be ressentiment plain and simple. For Nietzsche, revenge toward this world, toward the world of becoming, leads to a denial of life in favor of a transcendent, metaphysical world. However, for Heidegger, the metaphysical impulse has a deeper origin, one beyond sentiment and the reactive value creating will to power that remains merely some sort of coping mechanism of the weak. Heidegger sees the metaphysical impulse as not something to be disavowed, as did Nietzsche, but as something essential to the nature of human existence (Dasein). Heidegger thus takes the split world and metaphysics not as a mere fiction, but as a given, as an ontological fact of human existence.

Now what makes this fact of metaphysical transcendence possible is, for Heidegger, quite simply *nothing.* Nothing, or "the nothing" (*das Nichts*), is the very condition for metaphysics. In order for the human being to transcend to the metaphysical world, a space of nothing or *difference* must open up between the two worlds, between a being and its "being" or intelligibility. For example, when one attempts to think or understand a being, one must transcend or abstract away from that very being to that being's meaning or essence; this process of transcendence/abstraction (qua *thinking*) is occasioned by the space of nothing, or the space of difference. That is, the *why* itself arises by way of a "perceiving of nothing," a perceiving of the space between a thing and its intelligibility, which enables the very possibility of inquiry itself, insofar as all inquiry, all questioning, and thus all thinking, is meta-physics, as *meta ta phusika,* which is nothing more than transcendence itself.

Nothing, then, "grounds" metaphysics. Yet nothing is not a ground or a why in the metaphysical sense, but rather a nonground, an abyss (*Ab-grund*). This abysmal ground is "nothing" more than *beyng* itself. The nothing is beyng; beyng is the nothing. Heidegger often distinguishes beyng (*das Seyn*) from being (*das Sein*), the former being the condition for the possibility of the latter, where the latter is synonymous with a thing's beingness. Beyng then enables and conditions transcendence from a being (*das Seiende*) to its being (*das Sein*) or beingness (*das Seiendheit*).

Yet why does Heidegger equate beyng and nothing? Are these not the two most opposite concepts imaginable? What is their relation that makes them nearly synonymous? Heidegger's idea is that beyng and nothing are synonymous insofar as they are essential aspects of the same process or event (*das Ereignis*)—the event that enables metaphysics itself. The concept "is" is wholly dependent upon its opposite—"is not"—and vice-versa. Heidegger here follows Hegel in that pure beyng is indistinguishable from pure nothing; the terms only come to have any sense once they begin to buttress one another. Every "determination" is always a "negation," as Spinoza tells us. In other words, the very idea of "being" only arises from a transcending process occasioned by nothing, where beings are transcended to their being. Without nothing, then, being would be wholly concealed and ultimately unknowable. It is an awareness of nothing that makes human beings unique, insofar as nothing occasions the very possibility of abstract thinking and thus the human being as the rational animal.

Put another way, nothing allows for the being of beings to disclose itself in its truth, and this disclosure is the very process of truth as *aletheia,* and yet another facet of the being process. Here truth is understood in the verbal sense as *truthing,* as illumination or disclosure. Truth is simply the disclosure of a being in its meaning and, as such, is occasioned by the transcendence enabled by the nothing. If the nothing enables the illumination of a being's meaning by opening a space for this illumination to occur, then it could be said to enable this very illumination itself. Heidegger often thinks the notions of nothing as differential "space" and "illumination" together in what he calls the "clearing" (*das Lichtung*), which is intended to call to mind a clearing in a forest, where things become illuminated amid the surrounding darkness. Truth, beyng, and nothing, then, are all part of the same process known as the event. Additionally, Heidegger often speaks of this process, this event, not only as the truth of beyng and the event of beyng, but also as the essence, or essencing (*Wesung*) of beyng, by which Heidegger simply means that in this process, a thing's essence is able to be disclosed; that is, as a thing is transcended (by way of the nothing) toward its essence, its essence as its meaning comes to be illuminated (*truthed*), and thus a world, as a context of meaning, is opened up.

Although Heidegger's terminology is often obscure, essentially Heidegger has one thought in mind: beyng is the condition that enables things to be both intelligible and meaningful to us. Beyng, as the process of truth/nothing (i.e., clearing) enables a thing to be illuminated so as to become intelligible and meaningful. Metaphysics, beyond the mere philosophical discipline, and thought as "thinking" itself, is occasioned by beyng/nothing/truth. And yet it seems that in unearthing the "ground" of metaphysics qua transcendence, the condition for metaphysics as a philosophic discipline is also unconcealed. This condition, of course, is beyng as well.

Beyng, as the nothing, however, remains perpetually concealed from metaphysics itself; that is, beyng remains forgotten in favor of being, essence, and so forth. Moreover, beyng *eclipses itself* so that thinking as transcendence can occur. The "forgetting of beyng" is therefore the withdrawal of beyng *by beyng.* The onus is on beyng and not on the human being. This particular point will become important later as we discuss Heidegger's understanding of the sacred vis-à-vis the withdrawal of beyng that occurs with modern science and technology. The recognition of the concealed condition of metaphysics—beyng, nothing—already, in a sense, begins the process of "overcoming metaphysics," insofar as that which remains always concealed in metaphysics is finally revealed.

Now, in metaphysics, the concealment of beyng as its condition amounts to a kind of reductionism, where the meaning of beyng is reduced to one meaning, to one sense or showing, namely essence, ground, cause, and so forth. In metaphysics, the inquiry itself about beings is reduced only to the question of *what* or *why,* and this reduction ipso facto eclipses the deeper transcendental question of *how.* Thus, in uncovering this how, the reductionstic hold on metaphysics is lifted. Beyng can now show itself in "many ways," as Aristotle says. Rather than limiting being's being to essence as in metaphysics, a thinking into metaphysics' conditions transcends metaphysics and is a meta-metaphysics, which in turn opens up other possibilities, other possible ways for beings *to be.* As "being is said in many ways," none of these ways are reducible to a central meaning, as the "fundamental" truth of "what" beings *really are.* Rather, being discloses itself perspectivally, and can be thought from a myriad of perspectives. The reductionism of metaphysics, for Heidegger, reigns from Plato onward, even up to Nietzsche, who thought himself a perspectivist. According to Heidegger, Nietzsche merely reduced being to the subject and its value positing in will to power, a point I will return to momentarily.

Ultimately Heidegger argues that the human being itself is essentially meta-physical. That is, humans are unique insofar as they "think" and transcend beings to their intelligibility. The human being is essentially transcendence. Humans are aware of "the nothing" and thus are, by nature, metaphysics itself. Yet awareness of the nothing not only enables humans to transcend being, but also enables their own self-transcendence, meaning that humans can pass beyond themselves toward other "possible selves" or possible ways for them to be. Because of the nothing, we are able to conceive of *ourselves* in multiple ways and are able to continually make and remake ourselves. In other words, the beyng as the nothing enables our very freedom of choice. We can project ourselves into the future, and choose who we are to be. The human being, as this free being capable of metaphysical transcendence as well as self-transcendence, is what Heidegger means by Dasein. *Da-sein,* as the place where beyng happens, for Heidegger, means that human beings have the nothing within themselves, and are thus able to separate themselves from themselves, and thus *exist* in a unique way. *Dasein* in German simply means "existence," and no doubt Heidegger has in mind the Latin *ex-istere,* which means to "stand outside of." Dasein ex-ists, that is, exists in such a way that it stands outside of itself, ahead of itself, running-ahead to possible ways *to be.* "Metaphysics" is thus not, as it was for Nietzsche, an extrinsic conceptual framework that could simply be "overcome" by discovering its origins. Rather, for Heidegger, metaphysics proves to be what the human being essentially *is* at its core, namely transcendence.

However, for Heidegger, there remains an equivocation between metaphysics as the being that we ourselves are—Dasein—and metaphysics as the reduction of the meaning of being to a singular meaning. Dasein is metaphysics insofar as it transcends beings by way of the nothing, and yet "metaphysics" as a historical philosophical discipline has served not simply to transcend beings, but to transcend beings in such a way as to reduce their intelligibility to one sense. Because we transcend beings to their being, to their meaning, there is a tendency in us, and in being itself, for us to mistake *a* meaning of being for *the* meaning, that is, for us to mistake a singular *show-ing* of being for its only meaning, as in the Western metaphysical tradition, which mistook the meaning of being to be essentially *whatness.* Metaphysics in this reductionistic sense, for Heidegger, needs to be overcome.

The reductionism that is metaphysics is easy to see vis-à-vis modern, scientific conceptions of the human being. For example, conceiving of the human self as "just" a physical body made of neurons and brain chemistry would operate within a reductionistic and thus metaphysical framework (*Gestell*) for Heidegger. In fact, modern scientific and technological reduc-tionism remains one of Heidegger's primary opponents. In modernity, the human being, as well as "being" in general, is understood primarily in terms of the dominant metaphysical paradigm of science and technology, what Heidegger calls, again, the framework itself—the *Gestell.* In this framework, beings are reduced to one meaning: controllability; things *are* to the extent that they can be controlled, mastered, and dominated. This domination is confounded with knowledge (e.g., "knowing is power"), in that something is not considered to be "known" unless one can control and master it. For this reason, science remains slavish to technology and to the technological para-digm of mastery. Moreover, within this reductionist paradigm, the human being is conceived as "lord and master" of the earth, much akin to Descartes's famous saying from his *Discourse on Method* that human beings are to be "masters and possessors of nature." The human being, then, is the relegated to the sphere of mastery, as a master over nature and all that is; in short, the human being, the human subject, becomes "God."

Beings are reduced to one meaning, their manipulability, and the human being as the manipulator. This metaphysical paradigm of the framework therefore "crowds out" other ways in which beings—and human beings— can show themselves. The meaning of being itself is reduced to a singular meaning, and this meaning is none other than *will to power*. Heidegger therefore argues that the real underlying metaphysics to the modern paradigm of *Gestell* is Nietzschean will to power. Insofar as things *are* only to be dominated, and humans are the dominators, this amounts to the will to power's mastery, in the human subject, over becoming. The will to power, power itself, is the underlying metaphysics of modernity. Human beings, beings, and "being" writ large are all ultimately subservient to the paradigmatic understanding of reality in terms of power. Nietzscheanism then informs our very understanding of reality without our even being aware of it. For Heidegger, this Nietzscheanism is nihilism par excellence and constitutes the forgetting withdrawal of beyng itself.

Beyng has withdrawn and been forgotten, in that beings have only one meaning. Beings' polyvalence and multitude of possibilities have been closed off, concealed, and reduced to the singular meaning of power and manipulability. Beyng, qua truth as *aletheia,* as the illumination of beings in terms of their potencies, has itself been concealed. In each illumination or disclosure of a being in its meaning, other possibilities withdraw. This withdrawal of possibilities in favor of others is the essence of truth as revealing and concealing; that is, truth always illuminates and hides, discloses and conceals. Yet in metaphysics, especially modernity's metaphysics, concealment itself is concealed. In other words, the fact that beings have many meanings is hidden. For Heidegger, to "think concealment" simply means to understand the polyvalence of being's possibilities, that in every understanding of a being, another understanding recedes. Again this amounts to a kind of saturated perspectivism for Heidegger. Yet this perspectivism is, again, not on the side of the human subject, but rather beyng. The human subject does not determine or impose a being's meaning, but rather beyng shows itself in many ways.

Now what remains most interesting here from a Heideggerian perspective is not simply that beyng conceals itself, nor even that in metaphysics this concealment is concealed, but that beyng itself "shows itself" in a Nietzschean, subjective fashion. That is, beyng reveals itself *as if* the human being were the ultimate standard of value and that will to power were the meaning of beyng. If modern metaphysics is a reductionism that confuses human beings into thinking that they are the ultimate arbitrators of value—the ultimate lords and masters of nature—it is beyng itself that provides this confusion. In other words, the withdrawal of beyng *by beyng* leads to humans' self-deification in the metaphysics of will to power. Reality shows itself as if it were merely a blank canvas upon which the human subject is to paint meaning, as if it were essentially meaningless, and thus humans were the creators of all meaning. Things show themselves as if they were merely raw material to be formed in a *technological* manner. The brilliance of Heidegger's gesture here is that the onus is not on humans but on beyng.

For Heidegger, from this self-eclipse of beyng results considerable implications for religion and the sacred. Indeed, Girard follows the withdrawal of beyng as parallel to the withdrawal of the sacred. For Heidegger, the eclipse of beyng amounts to the eclipse or the "flight" of the gods and the holy, but whereas for Girard this is ultimately a positive movement in history, for Heidegger it is utterly nihilistic, and thus the greatest "danger" for Western culture. Given that beyng withdraws (or as Heidegger puts it in his *Contributions to Philosophy,* "abandons" us) and beings are reduced to a singular meaning, all other "meanings" of being are relegated to the "mere subjective." Art, poetry, religion, philosophy, and so forth are all considered to be subjective, aesthetic ways of considering the world that have ultimately no bearing upon what things *truly are.* The sacred, the holy, and religion in general especially then are consigned to mere subjective belief. The sacred ultimately has no place in our world. There remains no place for the sacred to appear, for all reality is reduced to raw material. In other words, the mysterious sacred dimension of existence is wholly concealed in the modern metaphysical paradigm of science and technology. For Heidegger, this is the true meaning of the Nietzschean "death of God." God's death is the nihilism of modern science and technology's dominant metaphysics of the will to power. The death of God then is tantamount to the concealing eclipse of the sacred itself.

Heidegger's project of overcoming or "twisting free" (*Herausdrehung*) of metaphysics, then, is not simply philosophical in nature, but also theological. Heidegger seeks to reinvigorate the sacred, to remythologize reality. This for Girard is nothing more than the resurrection and restoration of myth to its original place vis-à-vis the violent sacred. In what follows, we shall consider whether Girard's reading of Heidegger here is correct, that is, whether Heidegger does intend to resurrect the primitive, violent sacred and thus restore the mythic to its original place of prominence in human culture. Yet, given Heidegger's damning critique of Nietzsche and the metaphysics of the will to power, it will be anything but a simple fit between Heidegger and Nietzsche and Nietzsche's affirmation of violence and sacrifice. Heidegger's project, then, in the context of his critique of Nietzsche, proves much more complicated.

Girard's and Heidegger's Violent Sacred

As noted earlier, Girard's appropriation of Heidegger is similar to his appropriation of Nietzsche, insofar as Girard argues that Heidegger, despite being ultimately wrong in his understanding of the sacred, manages to come to an astounding insight. For Girard this key insight of Heidegger concerns his distinguishing between the Greek and Hebraic Logos within the context of the endeavor to overcome metaphysics. The decisive break with the metaphysical tradition occurs with regard to this distinction. For Heidegger, the break commences by leaving behind the corruptive influence of Christianity, whereas for Girard it is the complete opposite and inverse. Thus in what follows, I would like to detail more carefully Heidegger's and Girard's thinking on the overcoming of metaphysics vis-à-vis the proper understanding of Logos. As we shall see, each interpretation ultimately hinges on whether or not Christianity constitutes a regression or progression, and therefore on the notion of the sacred and its relation to the violence that ultimately follows.

Recall that Girard's hermeneutic seeks to interpret philosophy on the basis of religion, and not vice-versa, as it had been customary to do. For Girard, Greek philosophy, particularly the pre-Socratic Greek philosophy that Heidegger remains preoccupied with in his discussion on Logos, is a kind of abstraction from the religious. The Logos philosophy of the pre-Socratic

Heraclitus is indeed a theoretical mirror of the mythic sacrificial system. It is a mirror of the violent sacred. In Heidegger's reading, essential to the Heraclitean Greek Logos is *polemos,* that is, strife or quite simply *violence.* The Logos, from its original Greek root *legein,* means to "gather together," to unify, or to reassemble. Logos is the gathering of the *Hen-Panta,* the many into one. This idea of Logos is later expounded upon by Plato, who conceives of Logos as uniting the multitude of particulars together into one universal eidos or form. Yet this unification remains fundamentality a polemical and violent act, something altogether forgotten and concealed in its Platonic appropriation. "The *Logos* brings together entities that are *opposites, and it does not do so without violence.* Heidegger [therefore] recognizes that the Greek *Logos* is inseparably linked with violence."[1] For Girard, these opposites are nothing more than mimetic doubles, which are unified and brought to a relative harmony and stability by the Greek Logos as the *Hen-Panta.*[2] The Logos then prevents these opposites, now made similar as doubles, from completely destroying each other. Yet recall that the only way to prevent destruction among doubles for Girard is through the scapegoat mechanism. Thus this Logos for Girard is merely a theoretical abstraction of that very mythic mechanism. Girard writes,

> What is Heidegger demonstrating when he declares that not without violence does the Heraclitean Logos keep opposites together? Unsuspectingly, he is talking about the scapegoat and the way in which it engenders the sacred. It is the violence of the sacred that inhibits the doubles from unleashing even greater violence. The Heraclitean Logos, in Heidegger's terms, is the Logos of all cultures to the extent that they are, and will always remain, founded upon unanimous violence.[3]

The Heraclitean Logos, then, philosophically names the mythic activity or "logic" of scapegoating, in particular that unifying principle by way of violence that manages to stabilize a human community and prevent it from destroying itself. Girard's hermeneutic sees, in this Logos, an originary and concealed mythos.

That mythos and Logos belong together in an original unity, even in the Platonic dialogues themselves, has been noted by John Sallis in his *Being and Logos.*[4] Sallis's in this text argues that in every Platonic dialogue there remains a triangular relationship between mythos, Logos, and *ergon,* that is, the mythology, the philosophy, and the performance of the two in deed. Each Platonic dialogue then attempts to mirror in Logos and in deed a certain mythos and, accordingly, attempts a dialogue with a mythos itself. For example, Plato's *Phaedo,* a dialogue devoted to the question of the self or soul, seeks to establish a Logos of the soul vis-à-vis the Pythagorean and Orphic myths (represented by Cebes and Simmias of Thebes, pupils of Philolaus, the Pythagorean) of the transmigration of the soul in the context of the "deed" or act of the death of Socrates. Girard's argument, that a Logos would reflect and mirror a mythos, is therefore not something unique to Girard, but is indeed already operative, according Sallis, quite consciously, in Plato himself in his dialogues.

For Girard, the mythical and violent sacred is hinted at even further with Heidegger's remarks, in his *Introduction to Metaphysics* (1935), on Heraclitean *polemos,* as confrontation (*Auseinandersetzung*) and violence (*Gewalt*). Heidegger expounds upon Heraclitus's Fragment 53, which reads, "War [*polemos*] is the father of all and the king of all, and it has shown some as gods and others as human beings, made some slaves and others free."[5] Heidegger's exegesis of this passage concerns the way in which *polemos* as conflict and struggle creates a world, as an open relational context of meaning that establishes human beings and gods, as well as slaves and freemen. Because *polemos*—essentially violence—is "world forming," Heidegger says that *"polemos* and *logos* are the same."[6] Moreover, it is for this reason that Heidegger identifies the thinking of Heraclitus, the thinking that equates Logos with *polemos,* as ultimately *tragic.*[7] Heidegger thus reveals the Greek Logos to be both violent *and* tragic, and tragedy, as we have seen, is precisely the mythic sacred for Girard.

Like Nietzsche, Heidegger sees the need for an affirmation of violence as essential to a robust and complete theory of existence. Thus, Heidegger sees the tragic nature of Logos as consisting in the eternal struggle between being and seeming, between truth's revealing and concealing. Revealing and concealing exist in a *polemos,* a confliction-union between each other, and are both necessary for a complete picture of existence. It is only later with the Platonic metaphysical tradition that being is favored over the mere seeming of the Sophists. Moreover, Platonism's "metaphysics of presence" prefers to excise revealing from its essential concealing, and thereby begin the reductionism that is metaphysics itself.[8] For these reasons, Heidegger cites Sophocles's *Oedipus Rex* as an analogy to the true, complete, and tragic nature of existence as being composed of both being and seeming, revealing and concealing, and thus of Logos as *polemos*. For Heidegger, Oedipus seems innocent, but in the end must reveal his guilt, must unveil what is concealed. This unveiling is itself a violent act, and one that in turn leads to violence, the violence done unto Oedipus by himself.[9] The only way to endure such a disclosure of what he essentially *is,* that is, his own guilt, according to Heidegger, is for Oedipus to gouge out his own eyes. Oedipus's guilt, followed by his self-inflicted violence, tragically demonstrates the essential violence in revealing and concealing—in its movement from concealment to disclosure—and thus the violence at the heart of being itself. In other words, Greek tragedy highlights the fundamental violence at the heart of beyng's self-showing that at the same time conceals itself. Nevertheless, what remains interesting for our purposes is that Heidegger's conception of Logos as *polemos* follows Girard's, by its own admission, in its being essentially tragic.

For Girard, then, Heidegger unwittingly uncovered an essential insight regarding not only the Greek Logos, namely that it originates in violence, in *polemos,* but furthermore that this Greek, Heraclitean Logos remains sui generis, distinct from the Hebraic, Christian Logos. Heidegger argues that in the New Testament, particularly the Gospel of John, Logos means not the "being of beings" or the "gathering" of many into one, but rather *mesistes,* the mediator. Christ, as the Logos, is the mediator between God and human beings and as such is the "Word." This Hebraic Logos as word originates with the then-contemporary Jewish philosophy of Philo Judeaus, where the word in the Old Testament is that command or commandment (e.g., The "Deca-logue," or the Ten "Commands") which serves as mediator or messenger (*angelos*) between the two worlds. Indeed, Philo even speaks of the Torah, preexistent with God as the "only begotten Son." This Logos, which reaches its fulfillment in the Christian conception of Jesus as this "Son," has absolutely nothing in common with the original Greek meaning.

Here Heidegger's reading is quite contrarian with regard to the history of Christian philosophy and metaphysics that commenced in the second and third centuries and reached its climax in medieval philosophy, especially in the philosophy of Augustine and Thomas Aquinas. That is, the Christian philosophical tradition viewed the Greek conception of Logos as in a way prefiguring the Christian conception, the latter being a kind of fulfillment of the former. Heidegger seeks to expel the Christian notion of Logos and thus return to this original or "pure" sense of Logos as the gathering, by way of *polemos,* of the many into the one. In returning to this original sense of Logos, a deconstruction and thus overcoming of metaphysics can take place, leading to an original disclosure of beyng itself, namely beyng *as* Logos. In other words, Heidegger's task is fundamentally different from Girard's. Heidegger's task is to overcome metaphysics by investigating, historically, metaphysics' origins, its unthought conditions, which involves deconstructing the various historical conceptions of Logos with the hopes of returning to an original, fundamental meaning that can uncover an original Greek experience of existence. Heidegger believes he finds this original experience in the Greek Logos, and therefore must disentangle it from the Christian. Yet for Girard, Heidegger unintentionally uncovers in his finding of an original experience of Greek being an even deeper, hidden, and original experience of the sacred, namely the sacred as violence. In Logos as that unifying harmony which gathers opposites by way of *polemos,* violence, Heidegger uncovers the mythic sacred, and thus the original violence of the sacred itself. All is contained in Heraclitus's conception of Logos that Heidegger masterfully uncovers.

According to Girard, this uncovering leads Heidegger to *expel* the Christian Logos in favor of the Greek. That is, Heidegger argues that there really is no such thing as a properly "Christian philosophy," but rather simply an unoriginal appropriation of the Platonic and Aristotelian metaphysical tradition—what Heidegger terms ontotheology. Yet in saying this, with a stroke of irony, Heidegger uncovers the very meaning of the Christian Logos, not as mediator or messenger, or as some unoriginal distortion of Greek thinking, but rather as that which necessarily *must be expelled.* Indeed, it is the very essence of the Christian Logos to suffer expulsion; this is what makes it unique. If the Greek Logos is that which unifies through violence, the Christian, for Girard, is that which unifies by having violence done unto it. Thus the true Logos is directly wedded to its own *Passion.* Girard highlights three passages in the prologue of the Gospel of John that expose this expulsion of the Logos.

> In him was life and this life was the light of men. And the light shines in the darkness, *and the darkness could not comprehend it.* . . . He was in the

world, and the world was made through him, *the world did not recognize him*. He came to his own, *and his own did not receive him.* (John 1:4–5, 10–11, emphasis mine)

The Logos comes into the world and is not understood, recognized, or received. Rather, the Logos is rejected and expelled, tortured and crucified even. The Logos thus is the victim, the persecuted. It is that which violence is done unto, rather than in any way violent. Girard summarizes the Christian Logos concisely:

> The Johannine Logos is foreign to any kind of violence; it is therefore forever expelled, an absent Logos that never has had any direct, determining influence over human cultures. These cultures are based on the Heraclitean Logos, the Logos of expulsion, the Logos of violence, which if it is not recognized, can provide the foundation of a culture. The Johannine Logos discloses the truth of violence by having itself expelled.[10]

The Logos is therefore a "scape-*Logos*."[11] God is now understood to be the victim. The truth of human violence in itself and vis-à-vis God is now revealed.

Most importantly, the entire relationship between God and human beings is radically reestablished in this Gospel text. That is, what is revealed in this Gospel's prologue is that it is not God who expels human beings, but rather human beings who expel God. For Girard, John's prologue recommences the biblical meaning of the Fall in Genesis 3, not as God punishing and ejecting man from paradise, but rather man rejecting God. It is human beings who reject God, who are violent toward God, and not the other way around. For Girard, we are permitted to "correct the Bible only with the Bible" and thus are, in a sense, mandated to understand that John's prologue envisions an entire reversal to the original understanding of the relationship between God and human beings, rethought now from the *perspective* of the Logos as victim.[12] In other words, we are finally given the proper hermeneutic key with which to interpret not only the entirety mythology, but the entirety of the biblical tradition as well. The "Passion of the *Logos*" then reveals the true nature of human beings, but also the true nature of God; it is humans who reject God, and it is God who suffers violence at the hands of his own creation. It is God, as the Logos, who allows himself to be expelled so that the truth as to human beings and their God can be revealed.

Even Plato, who denudes the Logos of any remnants of its original Heraclitean violence, does not think of it as ipso facto being expelled. That is, for Plato, Logos functions as both a kind of intermediary between worlds, and a kind of gathering principle. It is Logos, for Plato, that gives us access to the world of Ideas. Thus Socrates can speak of his philosophical conversion in the *Phaedo* as a turning toward the *logoi* so as to glimpse the "truth of things" (99e–100a). Rather than looking directly at the truth, and risking "soul-blindness," as one risks being blinded by the sun, Socrates takes refuge in the Logos as a mediator between himself and the Ideas. Yet it is the Logos acting according to its etymological root of "gathering" that collects together many particulars into "one" and allows for a glimpsing of the many *as* one. Yet for Plato, this is anything but a violent act, as the world itself is already organized rationally; the Logos merely articulates what already *is*. The world is already naturally organized, the Logos merely carves the reality at its "natural joints" (*Phaedrus* 265e). For Plato, then, the Logos functions as both mediator and gathering, yet in a nonviolent way, or at least in a way that hides its violent origins. However, it seems that the only necessity for violence, for *polemos,* for Plato, would be if the world were not naturally organized, and thus would need to be violently gathered and collected. Plato's rational ontology of the Ideas avoids this very need for violent gathering. In other words, only in a Nietzschean metaphysics,[13] where the world is inherently meaningless, an amorphous world of mere becoming, would violence be necessary in order to form and organize it; indeed the act of "carving" by way of Logos would be among the most violent acts. Thought itself would be an act of violence. Whether or not Platonism simply overcomes the necessity of *polemos* within Logos by positing a rationally ordered world cannot as of yet be decided. However, we can note that the recourse for violence, at least metaphysically, is wholly contingent upon one's metaphysics, that is, whether the world is inherently ordered or disordered; if the latter, then violence certainly becomes a necessity. Platonism then marks the beginning of the removal of violence from Logos, and yet is still a far cry from the Christian notion of Logos as that which *eo ipso* must be expelled.

Heidegger's Logos and the Violent Sacred

The question remains as to whether there exists more evidence to link Heidegger's own conception of the holy to the violent sacred. Heidegger's dealings with theology and religion are always vis-à-vis the Platonic metaphysical tradition, which Heidegger regards, as we have seen, as a kind of degradation of an original experience of being. "Beyng" remains concealed in metaphysics, and with it a primordial experience of the divine. In reducing "beyng" to essence, and thus to mere "presence," the divine is only given a limited space in which to appear. This space is what Heidegger terms the ontotheological. For Heidegger, the ontotheological uncovers the essential connection between the metaphysical and theological reductionism inherent in Platonism. In short, for Heidegger, once the being of beings is conceived as "essence" and "ground" (these terms, for Heidegger, are functionally synonymous in metaphysics), once the many is "grounded upon" the one, then the question concerns the "manyness" of the "ones," which ultimately require grounding, an ultimate sort of grounding. This ultimate ground, as the ground of grounds and the essence of essences, is the functional equivalent of God. Metaphysics, then, thinks God as the highest ground, the ultimate "one," which is simultaneously the fullest meaning of "being" itself. For example, Aristotle's *Metaphysics* initially begins with an inquiry into being qua being, leading to discussions and distinctions between primary and secondary substance, the former being a "this," or composite of matter/form, and the latter being the mere form detached from the matter. Yet, as Aristotle's thinking moves into thinking these substances through the framework of act and potency, *energeia* and *dunamis,* ultimate "primary" substance becomes synonymous with immaterial substance, namely God. God "grounds" the causal chain of act/potency, halting an infinite regression. Ontotheology also affects Logos when it is interpreted as merely synonymous with *ratio,* as operating under a causal nexus with its categories of substance and causality. Thus, for Heidegger, once beings are conceived as substances within a causal nexus, ipso facto, this nexus leads (in order to avoid, again, infinite regress) to a terminus, in an unconditioned cause, that is simultaneously substantive in the highest sense. God here is the *ens causa sui.* In other words, the metaphysical conception of "being"—the onto-theo-logic—severely limits the way in which the holy can be conceived, even resulting in a kind of theoretical blasphemy. Heidegger famously writes that before this "God of the philosophers" one cannot properly dance or sing, as one could before the God of Abraham, Isaac, and Jacob.[14] Heidegger's theological challenge then, like his philosophical one of overcoming metaphysics, is the overcoming of ontotheology.

For Heidegger, a beginning to a way around ontotheology can occur by way of a deconstruction of Logos, as we have partially witnessed. Such a beginning occurs not only in his *Introduction to Metaphysics,* but also in a brief essay entitled "Logos" (from 1951). Here Heidegger reiterates that Logos is not immediately equatable with *ratio,* with reason, nor with *legein* as mere saying or speaking. Rather, Logos means primarily the gathering of the many into one. Yet Heidegger adds that this gathering into one is simultaneously a disclosure and concealing of that which remained concealed prior. That is, beings in their manyness remain in a certain way concealed and, thus, once they are gathered and collected, come to reveal themselves in another way. Thus Logos as this original gathering, insofar as it is simultaneously a revealing, is then also *truth* itself, truth as *aletheia*—unconcealment. "*Logos is in itself and at the same time a* revealing and concealing. It is *Aletheia.*"[15] Logos as *aletheia* is then a showing of beyng. It is a showing where beyng shows itself in a certain way, namely as one and as many. That is, beyng shows itself as it *is,* as a *one,* and yet as it *is not,* in the many, and, in turn, the one shows itself as itself, as it *is,* as *one,* and in the many, as it *is not.* It is a matter then of self-showing and concealing. If the one and the many are thought in terms of being and becoming, then via Logos being shows itself *as becoming* in the many, and becoming *as being* in the one. Logos therefore is the locus that unites these seeming opposites and oppositions, not just of the oppositions in manyness, but the primary opposition of one to many, which Logos unifies in terms of showings. Heidegger therefore writes,

> The *Hen-Panta* lets lie together before us in one presencing things which are usually separated from, and opposed to, one another, such as day and night, winter and summer, peace and war, waking and sleeping, Dionysus and Hades. Such opposites, borne along the farthest distance between presence and absence . . .[16]

It is then just as Girard noted, namely that all opposites are united together via Logos as the *Hen-Panta,* the "one-many," and this unification is synonymous with *polemos.*

Yet out of this polemical unification comes the theological. Heidegger notes another of Heraclitus's fragments (B 32): "The One, which alone is wise, does not want and yet does want to be called by the name Zeus."[17] Heidegger reads this dictum in light of his discussion of Logos and *aletheia* and understands Heraclitus to be indicating the self-showing of Zeus himself in and through the happening of truth in the Logos. Zeus shows himself in the very gathering activity that at the same time reveals—the "disclosive gathering." Heidegger speaks similarly in another lecture course on Heraclitus, where he notes that the gods themselves, as the *theoi,* are the ones who "look" at humans out of being, highlighting the etymological connection between *theos* as god and *theaon* as looking. Heidegger writes,

> Because the god is, as god, the one who looks, and who looks as the one emerging into presence, *theaon,* the god is the *daion-daimon* that in the look presents himself as the unconcealed. The one who presents himself in looking is a god, because the ground of the uncanny, Being itself, possesses the essence of self-disclosing appearance.[18]

The gods show themselves out of the happening of being, which is the happening of truth as unconcealment. This happening occurs too in the gathering activity of Logos, as Logos gathers via *polemos* the *Hen-Panta.* In other words, the Logos is a kind of site through which the activity of the gods can occur, an activity, we should be careful to note, that is always violent. "Zeus" then appears out of the polemical Logos and indeed both wants and does not want to be called *Hen,* or "the one." Heidegger quickly dismisses the eager identification of Zeus with the one as the impulse toward the ontotheologic. Here the one—as Zeus—is wholly excised and disconnected from the entirety of the Logos's activity of disclosive gathering. The tension, or we could say *polemos,* between the one's both wanting and not wanting to be identified as Zeus, needs to be kept alive and unresolved. Only then can Zeus appear *as* the one, or the one *as* Zeus, in and through the disclosive gathering, where many are revealed *as* one in a kind of divine activity. Heidegger notes,

The *Hen* is not apprehended as being by itself the *Logos*, if it appears rather as the *Panta, then* and only then does the totality of present beings show itself under the direction of the highest present being as one totality under this [unifying] One. The totality of present beings is under its highest aspect the *Hen* as Zeus.[19]

The one cannot be severed from the many, and given a status as the supreme one, the supreme ground, essence, or cause. Rather the one must appear *as* many, in and through the many, in a way that indicates the entire process of Logos qua truth, which is to show itself as under the direction of the highest being, the highest one, namely Zeus. In the simplest terms possible, I take Heidegger to mean that the entire process of Logos must be conceived as a divine activity and not isolated from any of its parts. This includes keeping the *polemos* or violence of the Logos as necessary to the divine process. In this way, then, we could say that here Heidegger broaches Girard's notion of the violent sacred, insofar as violence is indeed a necessary aspect of the totality of the divine activity. That is, insofar as *polemos* as violence remains inextricably bound to the disclosive gathering of Logos, and since Zeus, as the stand-in for the divine, can only authentically appear by way of the *entirety* of that process, the divine itself then remains wedded to the violent, and thus, for Girard, the violent sacred.

Yet Heidegger's *Introduction to Metaphysics* and "Logos" essay only begin his excursion into the theological. While these are the most important texts for Girard, there are others that are much more valuable if one is to decide Heidegger's conception of the divine, and whether or not such a conception is synonymous with Girard's violent sacred. In "The Origin of the Work of Art" (1936) Heidegger goes into further detail concerning the activity of *polemos,* Logos, and the appearance of the divine within the context of art as mimesis. Art is thought here, following Aristotle, as mimesis. Yet it is a strange mimesis, for it purports to imitate *nothing.* Thus, art in a sense is a kind of nonimitative mimesis, for Heidegger, that attempts to problematize the very idea of mimesis by making art imitate beyng as the happening of truth, something that does not preexist the mimetic act, but rather comes to be in the very act itself.

Heidegger follows Aristotle again in that art is not of the same kind of *mimesis* as, for example, history, which purports to accurately reproduce or mime particulars. Art represents, imitates, rather, the general essence of a thing (such a mimesis of essence would also be proper art in the Platonic sense). "The work, therefore, is not the reproduction of some particular entity that happens to be at hand at any given time; it is, on the contrary, the reproduction of things' general essence."[20] In other words, artistic mimesis *imitates* the universal, rather than the particular. And yet, for Heidegger, the true mimetic activity of an artwork does not imitate a pregiven universal or essence, but rather lets the very essence of the thing come into being in the mimetic act of the artwork itself. Therefore, in a sense, the artwork can be said to imitate *nothing*. Art imitates *the nothing*, that is, beyng as the happening of truth, disclosure. Art is a happening of truth, *aletheia*, an *event* of the disclosure of beyng. It imitates, therefore, that which only comes to be in the very occurrence of it. It is therefore a kind of reflexive mimesis. Art is, in short, an imaging of an original that is not pregiven, an original that does not exist prior to its imaging, and yet it is not as though the original is merely superfluous. On the contrary, the original, here the essence—the truth of beyng—is essential, as it pertains to the very nature of art. I call it therefore a reflexive mimesis precisely because it is mimesis that essentially *is* the activity of truth, and yet the mimesis is quite simply imitating itself as the *truth*. It is a self-imitative mimesis, for it images forth the very idea of imaging-forth. It is a disclosure *of disclosure itself,* a revelation of revelation, and so on. This revelation of revelation is, for Heidegger, nothing more than the shining of the beautiful itself.

Yet the mimesis of art is also an imaging-mimesis of *polemos,* or original strife (*Urstreit*). Art is ultimately the confliction-union of what Heidegger calls "earth" and "world," which comes to play and is imaged forth in the artwork. Earth and world are Heidegger's terms for his nonmetaphysical rethinking of the Aristotelian configuration of matter and form, respectively, though there is not simply a one-to-one correspondence between the two. Earth means simply the raw "stuff" of existence that always resists penetration and disclosure; in short, earth is always *concealed* and, accordingly, corresponds to *concealment* itself in the concealing-revealing that is truth/beyng. World, on the other hand, means the open relational context of meaning and thus corresponds to disclosure and *unconcealment*. World is the context of meaning as the environment of possibilities in which Dasein dwells. More importantly, earth and world exist in a *polemos* or strife that is imaged in the artwork. Yet this strife is grounded upon a more original strife between revealing and concealing that is the truth of beyng itself. Heidegger writes,

> Concealing denial is intended to denote that opposition in the essence of truth which subsists between clearing [revealing] and concealing. It is the opposition of the original strife. The essence of truth is, in itself, the primal strife in which that open center is won within which beings stand and from which they set themselves back into themselves . . . earth juts through the world and world grounds itself on the earth only so far as truth happens as the primal strife between clearing and concealing.[21]

Thus the original *polemos* that constitutes beyng/truth itself is imaged and mimicked in the *polemos* between earth and world. Therefore the artwork is nothing more than the *mimesis* of *polemos* itself. And since an artwork doubles back upon its own *mimesis* reflexively, the artwork is then *polemos* that imitates a more primordial *polemos*, a violent act that mimics *violence* itself as the heart of beyng. In other words, Heidegger's artwork reveals the *truth* about beyng; beyng *is polemos,* and thus beyng is, in a sense, *violence* itself. The artwork then is the locus for a kind of imaging of "mimetic violence."

Yet, for Heidegger, the artwork, as mimetic *polemos,* is also a disclosive gathering, a Logos. Indeed Heidegger again considers the interrelation between *polemos* and Logos, here explicitly in terms of the activity of *naming*. Heidegger writes,

> Language alone brings beings as beings into the open for the first time. . . . Language, by naming beings for the first time, first brings beings to word and to appearance. Only this naming nominates beings to their Being *from out of* their Being. Such saying is a projecting of the illumination [*Lichtung*], in which announcement is made of what it is that beings come into the open *as*. Projecting is the release of a throw by which unconcealment infuses itself into beings as such. This projective announcement forthwith becomes a renunciation of all the dim confusion in which a being veils and withdraws itself. Projective saying is poetry: the saying of world and earth, *the saying of the arena of their strife and thus of the place of all nearness and remoteness of the gods.* Poetry is the saying of the unconcealment of beings.[22]

Language as Logos in its nomination of beings *gathers* them together and, in doing so, illuminates them. This illuminative gathering is what first allows the appearance of not only beings, but beings *in their Being* as well and thus, as such, again, an appearance of the *Hen-Panta*. The one and many show themselves in the disclosive gathering of Logos. Logos allows for beyng to show itself as both one and many, that is, the one *as* many, and many *as* the one, each held in tension by the conflictual union that is *polemos*. Moreover, Heidegger names this "projective saying" (that is, the projection of *polemos* itself) the poetic—in an earlier draft of the essay Heidegger calls it *myth* (*Sage*).[23] The mythopoetic *says,* gathers, world and earth in their strife, and thus poeticizes not only their strife, but the original strife of beyng, which in turn opens a space for the "nearness and remoteness" of the gods. Again, the holy, for Heidegger, is explicitly linked with *polemos,* as struggle and conflict. It is out of the struggle and conflict of truth itself as a revealing that simultaneously holds back and withdraws that the mystery of the holy comes to presence and endures.

Earlier in the essay, Heidegger provides a concrete example as to how all of this works, or at least "worked" in the past, with his reflections on a Greek temple as a work of art. Here the temple is shown to be an image and thus an *imaging* of the god, which opens up a world, as a network of meaning, for a historical people. Heidegger reflects upon the conflict and struggle between earth and world in the temple that nevertheless are somehow unified and gathered together. Out of this struggle between earth and world, where earth always resists the illumination of world, the *claritas* of the beauty shines forth and makes the god himself present, and in a sense *is* the god himself. Heidegger writes,

> The temple, in its standing there, first gives to things their look and to men their outlook on themselves. This view remains open as long as the work is a work, as long as the god has not fled from it. It is the same with the sculpture of the god, a votive offering of the victor in the athletic games. It is not a portrait whose purpose is to make it easier to realize how the god looks; rather it is a work that lets the god himself be present and thus *is* the god himself.[24]

The temple as the space of the god is that which first gives things their "look" (*Gesicht*), that is, their eidos—essentially their essence or meaning. Moreover it gathers human beings, orients their lives, and gives them meaning. Finally the sculpture of the god is indeed an *image* of the god, and as such makes the god present, so much so that the sculpture *is* the god; indeed the sculpture, like the temple, is a disclosive mimesis of the holy that makes the sacred present. But Heidegger goes beyond the Greek temple and discusses the most powerfully sacred linguistic work of the Greeks—tragedy:

> The same holds for the linguistic work. In the tragedy nothing is staged or displayed theatrically, but the battle [*Kampf*] of the new gods against the old is being fought. The linguistic work, originating in the speech of the people, does not refer to this battle; it transforms the people's saying so that now every living word fights the battle and puts up for decision what is holy and what unholy, what great and what small, what brave and what cowardly, what lofty and what flight, what master and what slave (see Heraclitus, Fragment 53).[25]

Heidegger in this passage begins to tie together nearly every thematic element that we have discussed thus far. In tragedy, a struggle—*Kampf*—becomes present and even enacted among the people, a struggle that originally took place between the gods. That is, the tragedy, the "goat song," for Heidegger, is indeed a mimesis of an ancient sacred battle between the gods, which the linguistic now imitates and reenacts and, in reenacting, makes present again. Girard's understanding of myth and ritual illuminates this passage of Heidegger's quite nicely, as Heidegger seems to be indicating not only a sacred violence that names a "new god," what Girard would call a founding sacrifice, but also the ritual reenactment of that very sacrifice. In turn, this violence or struggle produces and delineates a world—"founds a culture," that is, delimits the gods and men, the masters and slaves, and so on, just as Heraclitus's dictum (to which Heidegger refers explicitly) originally spoke: "*polemos* is the father and king of all" (Fragment 53). It is understandable why Girard reads Heidegger's works as continually circling around the primitive sacred, as this passage bears all the marks of Girard's understanding of mythic ritual of "violence and the Sacred."

Does this then mean simply that the holy is linked undoubtedly with violence, as Girard seems to think? That is, is the holy, for Heidegger, really the sacred? Certainly if the holy remains inextricably bound together with *polemos* qua conflict or even struggle (*Kampf*), indicating a kind of violence, then Girard would indeed place Heidegger's holy within the category of the primitive and mythic sacred. Moreover, Heidegger's reading of tragedy as a kind of mythic, ritual mimesis of the gods' *Kampf* points to Heidegger's understanding of not just the holy, but beyng itself, as the mythic sacred. And yet *polemos* for Heidegger does not simply equate with the violent, at least in the Nietzschean sense of mastery and domination. As Heidegger notes, "We would surely all too easily falsify its essence if we were to confound strife with discord and dispute, and thus see it only as disorder and destruction. In essential strife, rather, the opponents raise each other into the self-assertion of their essential natures."[26] In this sense, Heidegger thinks of *polemos* as carrying the opposites in opposition beyond themselves, and thus of giving birth to something new, precisely, again, in terms of Girard's mythic sacred, which unifies opposites by way of violence. Furthermore, such violence and conflict giving birth new life is precisely in line with the Heraclitean fragment that names *polemos* as the "father of all," which even delimits the relation between gods and men and founds a culture. Heidegger is undeniably quite explicit in his favoring of this saying of Heraclitus as a proper explanation for the "worlding of a world."

In sum, Heidegger understands *polemos* and Logos synonymously, since Logos names the essential activity of the "conflictual union" of opposites, which are gathered together in order to appear. Logos is inherently polemical, and this polemical gathering that is at the same time disclosive names the very *event* (*Ereignis*) of beyng itself. Such a rethinking of Logos then leads to a rethinking of beyng, one that deconstructs and therefore twists free of the metaphysical reductionism that would seek to sever certain facets of the Logos so as to hierarchize them. *Polemos,* violence, therefore constitutes an essential aspect of Logos and thus an essential aspect of beyng, and therefore cannot be expelled without devolving to a kind of Platonism. Beyng is therefore tragic. However, in order to fully address the question of violence vis-à-vis the holy in Heidegger, we must turn now to his most sustained treatment of violence in *Introduction to Metaphysics* and to his most thorough discussions of the holy in his lectures on Hölderlin and his famous *Beiträge*.

Violence and Hölderlin's Holy

Heidegger's *Introduction to Metaphysics* devotes considerable time to discussing the meaning of violence (*Gewalt*) in the context of the Logos, *polemos*, and *deinon*, another Greek term Heidegger translates as both "violent" and "uncanny." A discussion of *deinon* arises out of Heidegger's glosses on Sophocles's *Antigone*. Heidegger interprets *deinon* when pertaining to the overwhelming nature of beings as the *uncanny*. The uncanny, in German *Unheimlich*, means literally "not being at home," or simply being ill at ease due to being displaced. Beings as a whole overwhelm human beings such that they feel displaced and not at home. Human beings then respond with *deinon*, with violence, as they form and mold the overwhelming nature of reality; this response constitutes the founding of a world, the worlding of a world, and it happens through poetry, language, thinking, and so on. "[Humanity's violence] gathers what holds sway and lets it enter into an openness. Humanity is violence-doing . . . it uses violence against the overwhelming."[27] This violence against "being" is the inception of culture, for Heidegger. It is a poetic act of *naming*, of Logos, and thus of gathering; yet this poetic gathering remains violence, insofar as the nature of the gathering is itself *polemos*. Moreover, this polemical-poetic act is what reveals beings as what they *are* and allows them to come to presence, that is, come to have meaning in a world. Heidegger will later refer to this violent act of the foundation of culture via the poetic act as the *event*, but here he refers to this as a "breaking forth."[28]

> This breaking forth, breaking up, capturing and subjugating is in itself the first opening of beings *as* sea, *as* earth, *as* animal [etc.]. A breaking-forth and breakup happen only insofar as the powers of language, of understanding, of mood, and of building are themselves *surmounted in doing violence*. This violence-doing of poetic saying, of thoughtful projection, of constructive building, of state-creating action, is not an application of faculties that the human being has, but is a disciplining and disposing of violent forces by virtue of which beings disclose themselves as such, insofar as the human being enters into them. This disclosedness of beings is the violence that humanity has to surmount in order to be itself first of all—that is, to be historical in doing violence in the midst of beings.[29]

Heidegger in this passage now furthers his understanding of the violence of human beings: it is only a response to the violence of being itself. That is, the disclosure of being is an event that humanity has to "surmount" in order to become itself, that is, becoming human. What is the human being? It is Da-sein, the place where being, the *violence* of being happens. This violence of being now is none other than *aletheia* itself, the disclosure of beings and their coming to have meaning in a world. The human being as Da-sein then partners with being, with *Sein,* so as to disclose a world and thus found a culture. Yet this disclosive founding is itself violent; it is violence itself. Logos, *polemos,* and *aletheia* then name the same reality: the event of the truth of being as it founds a world of meaning.

Violence is inherent to this process. Yet again, what does violence mean here? For Heidegger, as of yet, it is unclear whether this refers to bloodshed, to sacrifice, or to the common notion of violence, as we understand it. Perhaps Heidegger here is purposefully ambiguous. Nevertheless, it is quite easy to see how Girard's understanding of the violent origins of culture, the founding murder and its later eulogy in myth and sacrifice, and its later art form of tragedy, all echo in Heidegger's account here. Indeed, Heidegger explicitly links the violent founding of culture with the artwork, here thought through the medium of the Greek techne, as the violent setting into a work the violence of being itself. "Thus *techne* characterizes the *deinon,* the violence-doing, in its decisive basic trait; for to do violence is to need to use violence against the over-whelming: the knowing struggle to set Being . . . into what appears as beings."[30] Yet Heidegger further thinks of the relation of violence as a reciprocal relation between techne and *dikē,* or justice, which Heidegger translates as "fittingness" and which now stands for the overwhelming itself. That is, techne struggles against the fittingness of *dikē,* the fittingness of the overwhelming power of beings, and disturbs it; this disturbing is another way to think the founding of a world. In other words, the violence of the human being clashes with the fitting violence of reality, which, in turn, leads to the founding of culture in the poetic act that is simultaneously a Logos-*polemos-aletheia* and thus an artwork. "It is a matter of the inceptive, poetizing-thinking, ground and founding of the historical existence [*Dasein*] of a people."[31]

It is the opening of meaning, the founding of a world, that Heidegger thinks takes place in the poetic act of Logos, which is both violent (*polemos*) and disclosive (*aletheia*). This activity names the very *event* of beyng itself and thus unearths the conditions for the possibility of metaphysics, insofar as these are its very conditions. Heidegger shows that what metaphysics took to be hierarchical relations, for example, between the one and the many, are in their origin part of the same process, the process of beyng, and the coming to be of meaning. It is much like Heidegger's famous reflection on truth in paragraph 44 of *Sein und Zeit,* where Heidegger shows that before truth can mean anything like "correctness," or the proper correspondence of an idea to reality (e.g., the picture is on the wall), a world of meaning must first be disclosed and understood in which a propositional truth *could be* correct. Thus before truth is correctness, it is *aletheia,* or a disclosure of a world; *aletheia* stands as correctness's condition for possibility. So also it is with beyng itself, as the founding inception of culture, and the later metaphysical reflections upon such culture. Beyng stands hidden behind the scenes of the worlds of meaning we take for granted. Yet this beyng that remains hidden contains violence—in fact, *is* violence. In other words, the world is conceived by way of a hidden violence that is *named,* and in this naming a culture is "gathered."

Heidegger's reflections on Hölderlin's poetry further this understanding of beyng and the founding of a world and a people. However, now Heidegger thinks this founding explicitly with regard to the divine. Hölderlin's poetry then opens up for Heidegger an engagement with the sacred as it pertains to the founding of culture. For Heidegger, Hölderlin remains unique in this regard, for he is the only poet who poetizes about the *essence* of poetry itself, and therefore is a poet's poet.[32] That is, Hölderlin's poems act uniquely in naming the poetic act of beyng itself. Therefore Heidegger's choice of Hölderlin is not in any way arbitrary, but rather reflects the distinctive mark of Hölderlin himself as a poet of beyng and, as we shall see, a poet of the sacred.

The most important essay of Heidegger's for our purposes is entitled "Hölderlin and the Essence of Poetry" (1936). Heidegger first focuses his attention again on Logos, language, as both the "most innocent" and the "most dangerous" of all things. Again, Heidegger notes the dual nature of Logos as both creative and destructive. Moreover, language as Logos is thought as the *event,* the primary event (*das jenige Ereignis*).[33] This primary event occurs when human beings *name* their gods into being, into unconcealment. It is this naming that makes human beings unique, for human beings are a "conversation," that is, a historical dialectic based primarily in language and the nomination of gods. Indeed, it is language in this nominating capacity that is particular to the human being.

The history of human beings is the history of language, and this history is entirely contingent upon the naming of gods, which in turn founds a world. The human being then *is,* as such, in its capacity to *name the divine.* "Since we have become a conversation [*Gespräch*]—man has experienced much and named many of the gods. Since language has authentically come to pass as conversation, the gods have come to expression and a world has appeared."[34] And yet it is not as though a world precedes the naming of the gods, but rather the naming of the gods is the very worlding of a world. The appearance of the divine and a world are simultaneous and coterminous. Thus, the naming of gods as the worlding of a world, and vice-versa, is nothing more than the event of beyng itself. The disclosure of beings by beyng/truth remains contingent upon the "revelation" of the gods wrought by poetic naming, and thus this disclosure is wrought by the poets themselves. It is the poets who see the gods' "lightning flashes" and thus wrap "the heavenly gift in song" and deliver it to the people.[35] Human existence, at its core, is then poetic, for it is the poets who "stand in the presence of the gods" by way of their naming.[36] It is for this reason that poetry remains the most dangerous of occupations, for standing in the presence of the sacred, one is tempted to madness, as was Hölderlin. God's "excessive brightness drove the poet into darkness," claims Heidegger. Most importantly, because of this overwhelming danger that lies in poeticizing, the poet must therefore, for Heidegger, be *cast out.* Heidegger reads Hölderlin's line from his "Empedocles," "He must / Leave on time, through whom the spirit spoke," as Hölderlin's premonition of his own expulsion.[37] The poet needs to be expelled from the ordinary life so as to appear as if his occupation were riddled with danger.

I suspect Girard would read Heidegger's reflections here as the beginnings of the resurrection of mythology, a remythologizing about beyng and its poetic founding, and I am inclined to agree with Girard. Heidegger it seems is mythologizing the poetic act itself as a kind of tragedy, a tragedy where the poet himself must be expelled so that a world and culture may be founded upon the god's showing. This tragedy rests on the necessity of the poet's standing in the presence of the violent sacred and becoming expelled, cast out, in the naming of it. Heidegger's tragic mythologizing of beyng's "worlding" follows Girard's account of the mythic sacred perfectly, even with regard to the expulsion of the victim. However, in Heidegger's tragedy, the victim, the poet, is not so much guilty, but must appear "innocent," yet not innocent in any conventional sense, but rather innocent as a kind of harmless madness; the poet is made to appear mad and poetry to appear to be a "mere game." Such a false appearance is a kind of "noble lie" that remains necessary for the founding of culture. Thus Heidegger concludes,

> For how else could this most dangerous work be carried out and preserved, if the poet were not "cast out" of his ordinary life and protected from it by the appearance of the harmlessness of his occupation. Poetry looks like a game and yet is not.[38]

The poet then must be made to appear mad, fixated with a kind of game. Moreover, the poet must be exiled, exiled to what Heidegger calls the "in between," the space between gods and men. The poet's expulsion then is an exiling to the role of *mediator*, as the one who receives the god's "hints" (*die Winken*). Yet this exile accounts for a very specific time period and thus does not speak of some universal or timelessness; it is the time of the flight and arrival of the gods, that is, the withdrawal of the previous gods and the anticipation of the coming of the new god. It is a kind of middle period of messianism. "It is the *time of need* because it stands in a double lack and a double not: in the no-longer of the gods who have fled and in the not-yet of the god who is coming."[39]

Hölderlin names, for Heidegger, our current cultural climate, the climate of the wake of the death of God and the anticipatory hope of a coming god. Such quasi-messianism amounts to Heidegger's resurrection of the mythic sacred, a myth that attempts to speak of the *tragic* founding of culture based upon the expulsion of the one responsible for its very founding: the poet, who stands in the presence of the violence of the sacred and sacrifices himself so that this sacred can come to appear within a world.

Heidegger says little else in this essay concerning this tragedy and the kind of "god" he imagines to be coming. However, in another essay from within the same time period, "As When on a Holiday . . ." (1934/35), named after another of Hölderlin's poems, Heidegger discusses the nature of the "holy" as *to come* in more detail. Heidegger begins his reflections with nature (*phusis*) in its capacity to hold in unison opposites in their oppositions without, however, dissolving them. Nature is Logos in the sense of the polemical gatheredness. Heidegger equates this aspect of nature, namely the allowing for the buttressing of opposites to shine forth, with the beautiful. The confliction-union of opposites is the beautiful, which again reminds of Girard's violent sacred. "Beauty lets one opposite come to presence in its opposite; it lets their togetherness come to presence in unity, and thus it lets everything come to presence in everything, precisely where their differences are most genuine."[40] It is out of this unity-in-difference that the gods appear. In a way, then, Heidegger notes, nature is always morning, since it is always "to come." Moreover, the poets, as the "ones to come," are always in anticipation of nature's coming, and indeed measure their being in terms of their anticipation of the "essence of nature."

The essence of nature is *phusis,* as the ever emerging into disclosure that illuminates beings in their meaning and thus "worlds a world." It is an "emerging and an opening," that is, it is a clearing.[41] In other words, Heidegger now thinks *phusis* as beyng, as the coming to be of meaning by way of the illumination of a world. Nature is a kind of continual springing forth of meaning that is always to come and never exhausted, and therefore can always be anticipated by poets, as it is ever rich in meaning. Yet as the poet feels the coming emergence of nature, he names nature as "the holy," for nature's essence *is* the holy. The holy is the "strife" or violence of beyng itself as the violence between revealing and concealing, as we saw in the artwork essay. Thus at the core of the holy is chaos; indeed, the holy is chaos, and emerging out of the chaos. Indeed it is out of this primordial chaos that is the holy that the gods appear and appear in their relation to men. The holy is thus "timeless"—although Heidegger is quick to note not in any "Christian sense"—and prior to even gods, as it remains the eternal chaos itself, which gives birth to the gods and men and their interrelation in a world. It is, again, the primordial *polemos,* as Heraclitus names "the father and king of all," which grants to men their rank, thus opening a context of meaning. The holy is then the "terror of complete shock."[42]

Additionally, Heidegger goes through great pains to interpret the Hölderlin's poem ("As When on a Holiday . . ."), as anti-Christian, particularly the part concerning the "suffering god." The lines in question run as follows:

Yet us it behooves, you poets, to stand
Bare-headed beneath God's thunderstorms,
To grasp the Father's ray, itself, with your own hands,
And offer it to the people
The heavenly gift wrapped in song
For only if we are pure in heart,
Like children, are our hands innocent.
The Father's ray, the pure, does not sear it
And deeply shaken, sharing a god's suffering,
The eternal heart yet remains firm.

Rather than interpret this in a Christian manner, Heidegger under-stands Hölderlin to be speaking of the holy's very "sending" of itself, via its "ray," which is named as a god by the poet, and which, in turn, threatens the very essence of the holy itself. That is, the holy's self-bestowal means a self-inflicted suffering it must undergo in order to communicate itself with humans by way of the mediation of the god and the poet. Heidegger's prose is quite obscure, but he seems to imply that the holy, which stands immediately with itself, threatens its very nature in its attempting to reveal itself. And yet, in the end, since the holy reveals itself to be primordial suffering, as it is primordial strife, it is in the holy's very nature to threaten itself, to hold itself in opposition with itself in its self-suffering. Heidegger surmises,

> By offering itself to the decisiveness of the ray that is a suffering, the holy
> nevertheless abides, the radiating in the truth of its essence, and so it suffers
> primordially. Yet since this originary suffering is not a sacrificial tolerance,
> but instead the intimacy that gathers everything to itself, it does not share
> the god's suffering in a pitying and compassionate way. Suffering means to
> remain steadfast in the beginning . . . it is the coming of a beginning.

If we understand the holy here to be *phusis,* beyng, as the happening of truth, then we can interpret Heidegger to be saying that the self-emergence of *phusis,* the disclosure of a world of meaning, constitutes a primordial bestowal of beyng itself, and, as such, a primordial "suffering," which ought not to be "pitied," but rather endured. In other words, beyng as the *polemos-*Logos-*aletheia,* in founding a culture, always involves suffering, for it always involves a kind of self-sacrifice of the holy. Beyng must "send" itself violently and await a violent act of naming—techne—and thus emerge into presence. Beyng then is essential "tragic activity," which must undergo violence in order to bestow itself, in order to let beings *be*. In Girardian language: such self-sacrificing of the primitive, violent holy presents a mythology of beyng that likely echoes an originary murder. Indeed, Heidegger says as much, insofar as he likens the holy to an essential, originary suffering that constitutes its very essence in its self-bestowal.

It is worth noting that Fr. William Richardson reads this passage as naming the essential risk involved in the beyng process itself, namely that it be mistaken for a being, and thus mutatis mutandis the holy be mistaken for a god.[43] Richardson then understands this passage within the larger Heideggerian framework of the metaphysical reduction of the meaning of being to one meaning, one showing, essentially mistaking *a* showing of beyng with *the* showing. This reductionistic element, as we saw, is the heart of metaphysics as a historical disciple, for Heidegger, and now, according to Richardson, it also applies to the holy, the worry being that the holy be confused with some historical showing of itself, and thus run the risk of being itself forgotten. It is a matter then of recognizing that, like beyng, the holy *always* recedes in favor of the gods, and thus to mistake the holy for a god would be blasphemy. I agree with Richardson that this element of antireductionism vis-à-vis the holy is certainly present and on Heidegger's mind in this essay. Nevertheless, there still seems to be elements of Heidegger's reflections that go beyond this and point instead to an essential violence, a self-violence and thus self-suffering, at the heart the holy in its own self-bestowal. Rather than conceding to Hölderlin's Christianity in this stanza, Heidegger instead does mental gymnastics to make it fit within his ontology.

Heidegger concludes the essay by speaking of the holy as that which "calls" and "hints" to the poet, who then anticipates its coming. Indeed, the holy is synonymous again with the messianic "to come." For Heidegger, this unique period in history where we are "between gods," between showings of the holy, calls the poet to anticipate the coming of the holy in a way that would anticipate a crossing to a "new beginning." In the *Contributions to Philosophy,* Heidegger will think this coming holy under the name of the "last god," which signals a showing of the holy that entirely enables an overcoming of metaphysics, Christian metaphysics in fact. The last god will call to the human being out of the "abandonment" of beyng (by beyng) and necessitate a distressed turn toward the god in anticipation of its coming, which will ground an entirely new culture, one that has foregone metaphysics. Heidegger writes, in sum,

> In its coming, the holy, "older than the ages" and "above the gods," grounds another beginning of another history. The holy primordially decides in advance concerning men and gods, where they are, and who they are, and how they are, and when they are. What is coming is said in its coming through a *calling*. Beginning with this poem, Hölderlin's word is now the calling word. . . . The holy bestows the word, and itself comes into this word. *This word is the event [Ereignis] of the holy.* Hölderlin's poetry is now a primordial calling which, called by what is coming, says this and only this as the holy. The hymnal word is now "necessitated by the holy [*heiliggenöthiget*]." (Emphasis mine).[44]

All of this speaks to what seems to be Heidegger's understanding of beyng as essentially "tragic."[45] Indeed in his *Besinnung,* Heidegger not only notes that the great fundamental poetry is tragic, but that tragedy itself occurs out of the "essence of beyng."[46] Moreover, philosophy itself—as the meta-metaphysical philosophy that thinks beyng as to its essence and its truth, that is, the coming to be and disclosure of a world—is itself tragic. "'The philosophy of the tragic' says the same thing twice" and thus is a redundancy for Heidegger, for the inquiry into beyng is an inquiry into the tragic, for beyng is itself tragic. Yet what exactly could this mean? Although Heidegger himself is not explicitly clear, given his understanding of the nature of meta-metaphysical philosophy (what he will later call simply "mindfulness") as well as the nature of beyng itself as a disclosive and polemical gathering, it seems that the tragic names simply the self-expulsion of beyng itself *by itself.* Beyng must withdraw in favor of beings; it must conceal itself. Furthermore, the thinker called to think this self-expulsion must also become a tragic figure, risking expulsion himself by being misunderstood. In his *Beiträge,* Heidegger comes to equate Dasein with the poet as the "one to come" who will anticipate the call and hint of the holy. That is, in the *Beiträge,* Dasein is no longer the "being that we ourselves are," but rather a poetic existence that the human being is called and beckoned to by the holy itself as the last, ultimate god (*der letzte Gott*). Thus the thinker and the poet become synonymous, insofar as they are called to ground a world by naming a new god—the *last* god. And yet, according to Heidegger's contemporaneous lectures on Hölderlin, the poet always must be "cast out" as mad and his work as insignificant, a fate the poet himself must suffer for the sake of his disclosive naming of the god into being. Therefore, for Heidegger, both beyng and the poetic-thinker who responds suffer a tragic fate and are therefore themselves a kind of tragedy.

However, recall that the thinking that would get beyond metaphysics does so first by deconstructing metaphysics as to its conditions; then and only then can metaphysics be transcended. And yet, for Heidegger, a thinking that unearths metaphysics' conditions already has, in a sense, traversed to an "other beginning," one beyond metaphysics:

> *The question,* what is metaphysics?, already inquires into what is essential to "metaphysics" in the sense of gaining an initial footing in crossing to the other beginning. In other words, the question already asks from within this other beginning. What it makes visible in its determination of "metaphysics" is already no longer metaphysics, but, rather its overcoming.[47]

In other words, the kind of thinking that inquires into metaphysics' conditions has already transcended metaphysics insofar as it thinks and *names* beyng. The question now remains as to whether or not this naming of beyng as the unthought ground of metaphysics amounts to a tragic thought. Certainly metaphysics suffered under the yoke of a tragic fate, insofar as it began with an initial "forgetting" of the withdrawal of beyng itself, and thus was forced to play this "concealed concealment" out throughout the philosophical thinking of the West in various instantiations of being as essence, ground, and so on, until it finally exhausted itself with Nietzsche. It stands to reason that Heidegger (and we can only speculate) would view this history of metaphysics as a kind of tragic fate. Indeed, Heidegger often refers to the history of beyng as a kind of "fate" (*das Schicksal, das Geschick*).[48] For recall that even the tragic fate of metaphysics is "sent" (*Geschickt*) by beyng itself. That is, the eclipse of beyng is a self-eclipse self-wrought by beyng, which finally exhausted itself in the "showing" of itself as a mere vapor in Nietzscheanism, where the human being thinks himself "master and possessor" of nature.

However, given that the thinking that overcomes metaphysics recognizes the tragic fate of beyng, that beyng always expels itself, does this then mean that the thinking of the "other beginning" somehow twists free of tragedy itself in the very recognition of itself? Much as, for Girard, Christianity illuminates the mythic sacred and its scapegoat mechanism for what it is, so too, by analogy, the thinking that transcends metaphysics now recognizes the necessary self-expulsion at the heart of the nature of beyng. There remains then an important parallel between Heidegger and Girard vis-à-vis the illumination of the expelling at the heart of beyng and at the heart of the sacred, respectively. However, this parallel, it seems, is as far as it goes, for violence still rests at the heart of beyng, of Logos, for Heidegger, and thus cannot be reconciled to Girard's understanding of the Christian Logos, which wholly twists free from violence. Moreover, Heidegger's holy—the last god—is "the entirely other against all previous gods, especially against the Christian god."[49] By this statement, and others like it, Heidegger takes a firm stance against Christian thinking *insofar* as it always remains wedded to Platonic metaphysics, which Heidegger believes inevitably led to the domination of nature via modern technology's Nietzschean metaphysics. For these reasons Girard sees Heidegger's thinking as unknowingly describing the retreat of the primitive sacred under the guise of beyng in replace of the slow progress of the Christian, nonviolent holy.[50]

Heidegger's criticisms of Christianity appear to have remained with him his whole life, even when his thinking moves from a more active, *polemos*-centered nature (e.g., 1930s) to a more passive, receptive nature (1950s and onward). John D. Caputo recognizes three phases, or "turns," in Heidegger's thinking: (1) from Catholicism to Protestantism (1917–1919), which one sees in Heidegger's Marburg and Freiburg periods, and which culminates in *Sein und Zeit;* (2) a turn toward heroic voluntarism lauding Nietzscheanism (1928–1929); and (3) a move beyond Nietzscheanism to a mythopoetic meditation upon the gods and the holy, a kind of neopaganism, which ultimately culminates in Heidegger's thinking on *Gelassenheit.*[51] However, given our previous reflections, it seems that this threefold division will not suffice in terms of the heart of the matter, namely Heidegger's relation to violence. That is, it seems a more radical *Kehre* occurs once Heidegger begins to break with his obsession with *polemos* at the heart of beyng, something that still preoccupied Heidegger throughout the 1930s and into the early 1940s.

I have suggested elsewhere that a beginning "turn" in Heidegger occurs between his first and second Nietzsche lectures (circa 1936), where Heidegger begins to view Nietzsche in a more negative light, eventually holding him responsible for the metaphysics of modern technology.[52] As Heidegger begins to break with Nietzsche, his thinking becomes much more passive, focused on themes such as "shepherding beyng" and the "meditative thinking" of "letting-be." Indeed, Clare Geiman follows this path to Heidegger's thinking vis-à-vis his concept of techne, which includes *deinon*, from *Introduction to Metaphysics,* and how such a concept becomes almost wholly denuded of the violence it once possessed.[53] Geiman marks this break sometime around 1942 with Heidegger's rereading of *Antigone* in the context of more Hölderlin reflections ("The Ister"). Geiman even notes Heidegger's own retraction of his initial identification of Hölderlin's poet with Nietzsche's Übermensch, arguing that the latter is anti-Greek and rooted in the metaphysics of will to power.[54] For Heidegger, techne is no longer thought as a violent (*deinon*) activity that harnesses the "overwhelming" violence of nature itself, but rather a meditative thinking that "lets be" by willing to not-will. *Gelassenheit* remains wholly antithetical not only to violence, but to any trace of a "metaphysics of the will" that one finds so enmeshed in modernity's Nietzschean metaphysics of the will to power. *Gelassenheit* names the complete antithesis to the will to power and its violence toward nature in the form of the *Gestell* and its reductionistic framework that seeks to reduce beings *so as* to master and control them. Indeed, it seems Heidegger's so-called *Kehre* is best thought in terms of a turn away from violence to antiviolence. Such a reading of Heidegger is quite compatible with Richardson's understanding of Heidegger-I and Heidegger-II as a turn from Dasein to *Sein,* although Richardson marks this break much earlier (1930) with "On the Essence of Truth."[55] Moreover, in a footnote, Richardson makes the claim that it is perhaps possible to understand Heidegger's *Kehre* in terms of tragedy: "Wouldn't it be a delicious irony to take this as the *point de depart* for another study of Heidegger-I considered as the philosophy of 'tragic existence,' as seen by Heidegger-II?"[56] In other words, Richardson recognizes the early Heidegger as obsessed with beyng as tragic, and the later Heidegger as a move away from tragedy—and violence—into the thinking of *Gelassenheit.* This move away from the violence-centered thinking of the 1930s is precisely what Girard and other thinkers like Gil

Baillie fail to consider, and yet both remain correct in that this retreat from violence nevertheless maintains its attack on Christianity.[57]

Ontotheology versus the Violent Sacred

Although Heidegger does perhaps move away from violence and tragedy, his criticisms of Christianity never cease. Heidegger even in his later thinking still seems to understand Christianity as ontotheology and thus wedded to Platonic metaphysics, which eventuates in Nietzscheanism. Indeed, Heidegger contends that understanding the world as *created,* implying a *creator,* is precisely what leads to the modern metaphysics of technology, for once God "dies," the *creator/created* or *producer/produced* metaphysics still remains, albeit with the human subject in the place of God. It is precisely this understanding of beings as "things produced" for which Heidegger faults Christianity.[58] That is, Christianity is rooted in a productive, technological comportment of the human being that now deifies the human being as the master of nature. Heidegger, then, still maintains his critique of techne and violence, but now applies it to Christianity as the metaphysical root of such violence. This amounts to the heart of Heidegger's ontotheological critique, which blasphemously eclipses the true holy in favor of a theoretical distortion. Heidegger argues that simply conceiving of God as "creator" in the Judeo-Christian sense is already a distortion and assault on the holy.[59] One immediately suspects a bias here on the part of Heidegger in his arguing that there indeed exists a "straight line" from conceiving of God as creator and things as *ens creatum* to the metaphysics of the will to power in modern technology. Granted, there is certainly a consistency in logic between the two, and one can imagine how the death of God could precipitate this outcome. However, while the "logic" remains present between Christianity and *Gestell,* it is a far cry from Christianity's necessitating it. Such necessitation, it seems, can only be argued by considering this "logic" from an amoral perspective, where violence constitutes the essence of thought itself—what is sometimes called by deconstructionists *logocentrism.* Similar to Nietzsche's argument, Platonism (and Christianity as its herald) would have to necessitate a kind of "fascism of truth" that would eventuate in violence, if and only if theoretical thinking itself were considered to be ipso facto violent. We touched upon this earlier when considering Arendt's critique of the "techne model" of politics, which seeks to stamp reality, fascistically, with *the* Truth, in a way similar to the artisan who looked to the world of the Forms so as to then form the material its image. Heidegger himself makes precisely this argument very early in his *Basic Problems of Phenomenology* course, where he notes that the metaphysical impulse itself arises from a *technological comportment* of Dasein.[60] Thus it seems Heidegger implicitly at times, like Nietzsche, calls into question the very nature and function of reason itself as perhaps inherently violent.

Interestingly enough, neither Heidegger nor Nietzsche (nor even Kant) was the first to call into question *ratio* as not only violent, but also blasphemous. Martin Luther in his reformational attack on Catholicism and its *theologiae gloriae* dubbed reason "the Devil's whore," which must be slain for the sake of Christ and his *theologiae crucis.*[61] Moreover, Luther's attack on *ratio* amounts to an attack on *essentialism* and is thus a proto-critique of the "metaphysics of presence" that we find in Heidegger and Derrida. In a famous passage from his *Lectures on Romans,* Luther advocates for an antiessentialist position that would favor beings not as they *are,* but rather as they *will be:*

> Learn from the apostle to consider the whole creature as it waits, groans, and travails in pain, i.e., as it turns with disgust from what now is and yearns for what is to come. Then the science of the essence of things and of their accidental qualities and differences will soon become worthless . . . anyone who searches into the essences and functionings of the creatures rather than into their sighings and earnest expectations is certainly foolish and blind.[62]

Luther's critique here goes beyond a critique of merely "natural theology" and cuts to the heart of the matter, namely metaphysics itself as a theory of essences, grounds, causes, and so on. The "madness" (as Luther terms it) of theoretical speculation must be replaced with a theology of *anticipation* that "yearns for what is *to come*" in *apokaradokia* ("eager expectation"). Indeed, Luther translates *apokaradokia* (from Romans 8:19, "the creation waits in *eager expectation* for the sons of God to be revealed") as ängstliche Harren, that is, anxious waiting or anticipation. It is reason, along with its metaphysics of essences, that must undergo a theological transformation.

Luther's critique, along with Heidegger's, seems, however, to create as many problems as it solves. First, any critique of reason (*der Grund*), as we have seen, is necessarily a critique of cause (*der Grund*). This critique of cause has considerable repercussions with regard to the traditional doctrine of the "analogy of being," which assumes creatures stand in relation to God by way of an analogy, where strictly speaking the only thing known of this analogy is that the relation stands as one of *cause* to *effect*. That is, although we know nothing of the divine *esse*, as to *what* God "is" in himself, we can know *that* God is and *positively* predicate of God by analogy, namely the analogy of cause to effect. This doctrine allows then for more than mere "negative theology," as it attempts to positively predicate of the divine. For example, God's goodness and creaturely goodness are said analogously, as God's goodness remains ultimately unknowable, save as we understand God's goodness to *cause* and *ground* all creaturely goodness. Since we know what creaturely goodness is, we can thus know that God is good, albeit to an exponentially greater degree, insofar as God is the ground and cause of such goodness. In other words, creaturely goodness *participates* in the goodness of God, as its cause. So although we cannot know what it means for God to be "good," we can know that he *is* good, by analogy. Yet if we were to take away the cause-effect relation, the doctrine of analogy would falter, and negative theology, at best, would ensue. God would remain wholly *unknowable*, even with regard to his goodness, love, and so on, and would thus be, in a sense, *beyond good and evil.*

Such a God beyond good and evil is where a destruction of ontotheology inevitably leads, for it would remain impossible to predicate *essentially* concerning the divine "nature." Terms such as "essence" and "nature" must be foregone, as God cannot be bound by any essential nature. Thus, for Luther, essentialism is replaced with a radical volunteerism, where God's "will," whatever that may be, is "good." "God wills it so and because he wills it so, it is not wicked."[63] God remains no longer subject to our rational categories of goodness; thus any action could perhaps be called "good," so long as it comes from God, even actions that humans perceive to be intrinsically evil, even violent actions. Indeed such a critique of essentialism allows for violence to enter into the Godhead once more. Kierkegaard's *Fear and Trembling* famously explicates this implication in his analysis of the "binding of Isaac," where God is entitled to "teleologically suspend" the ethical, since the divine nature is paradoxical, absurd, and thus beyond rationality. We must therefore ask: does any critique of rationality vis-à-vis the divine result in an inevitable resurrection of the mythic, violent sacred, insofar as it reinserts violence back into God's will? Can we date this resurrection beginning with Luther?

Luther's primary task, as a reformer, but also as a philosopher and theologian, was to deconstruct Christianity's unholy marriage with Greek metaphysics, particularly Aristotelianism. As shown above, Aristotle's *Metaphysics* and its essentialism proved to be considerably problematic for Luther; however, even more so was Aristotle's *Ethics,* which, for Luther, dictates a "works-based" theory of salvation, of becoming "righteous" (*dikeō*), due to Aristotle's emphasis on the habituation and inculcation of habits. "The righteousness of God must be distinguished from the righteousness of men which comes from works—as Aristotle in the third chapter of his *Ethics* clearly indicates. According to him, righteousness follows upon and flows from actions. But, according to God, righteousness precedes works, and works result from it."[64] Thus one becomes, according to Luther's Aristotle, good by practicing goodness, and righteous by practicing righteousness. For this reason, Luther decreed Aristotle's ethic to be antigrace, as it supposes justification (*dikaiōsūnē*) to be based on human effort rather than grace of God. Indeed, if one were to distill all of Luther's theology into one idea, it would be *sola fide,* or "justification by faith *alone.*"[65] Thus Luther writes that "the whole Aristotelian ethic is grace's worst enemy," for it places the *power* of salvation into the hands of the human being.[66] Rather, for Luther, the human will is utterly *impotent,* enslaved to sin, and thus unable to save itself, which leads Luther to a kind of radical determinism where anything like "free will" certainly does not exist. However, with no free will, how then does one come to choose the salvation that is by faith alone? Luther ultimately places the burden of the problem of salvation upon God's election, arguing for a radical version of predestination, likened to late Augustine or Calvin.

Now, Luther's critique of free choice of the will results in radical implications with regard to the so-called problem of evil. For if humans possess no such free will, then neither are humans responsible for any evil. For Luther, the origin of evil resides rather in God's "hidden will" (as opposed to his "revealed will"), which imprisons humans in disobedience, hardens their hearts, and thus even wills humans' eternal damnation.[67] Thus Luther is just as much, if not more, of a "Calvinist" than Calvin, concerning predestination.[68]

This concealed and hidden will of God lies outside the grasp of human *ratio* and thus determines what we consider to be "good" and "evil." Evil, violence, and so on, reside in the hidden, concealed will of the Godhead, or perhaps we should say, the sacred, since such a reinsertion of evil and violence into the divine is precisely that of the mythic, violent sacred. It seems then that Luther's intentions of rescuing Christianity from Hellenism result, in a way, in a deeper enmeshing within it, insofar as *sola fide* leads to radical human impotency, and impotency to a reinscribing of violence within God. Therefore Luther writes, "It is true that God wills evil and sin."[69]

In Heidegger's famous postwar "Letter on Humanism" (1946) he again speaks of the essence of evil as belonging to the essence of beyng itself, namely beyng's truth as the process of revealing and concealing. "Evil appears all the more in the clearing of being. The essence of evil does not consist in the mere baseness of human action, but rather in the malice of rage. Both of these, however, healing and raging can occur only essentially in being. In it [evil] is concealed the essential provenance of nihilation."[70] In other words, like Luther, the essence of evil is to be located from within being, and not from within human volition. Evil occurs as a necessary consequence of the concealing and withdrawing nature of beyng that conceals itself so as to let beings be. It seems then that a necessary consequence of beyng's "letting be" is, at times, the "malice of rage." As late as 1946, Heidegger thus still speaks as though evil and violence (here rage and malice) were part of the essential constitution of beyng itself. Moreover, like Luther, Heidegger seemingly exculpates human beings (certainly himself, at least) from the responsibility of evil and violence.

The critique of essentialism in ontotheology, however, need not necessarily lead to an "ontology of violence" or an extreme voluntarism concerning the divine. For example, Richard Kearney and John D. Caputo choose, in light of this antiessentialism, to place the burden of evil on human beings, thereby rendering God effectively "weak" and impotent.[71] For Kearney, for example, God can only "be" in this world by way of human concession and permission. That is, rather than rendering human agency impotent, Kearney chooses to place powerlessness upon God, in order to "solve" the problem of evil. Indeed, for Kearney, God is not to be identified at all with *being* or *existing,* but rather with sheer *possibility* and *potency.* In this way, the problems that antiessentialism brings—God's being "beyond good or evil"—can be circumvented. Yet the problems remain for any critique of ontotheology, insofar as such a critique ipso facto ruptures the analogy of being, and thus the hierarchy of essences, and results in subsequent problems with regard to the nature of violence and evil in reality.

The question of essentialism vis-à-vis the divine goes back as far as Plato's *Euthyphro,* which investigates whether gods transcend or are subject to essences. While Plato ultimately argues in favor of the latter—indeed even arguing to ban tragic poets from the city to safeguard this notion of the gods, it is Aristotle who finally identifies God with the good itself (*Metaphysics* 1072b). For this reason, and rightly so, Heidegger labels all subsequent metaphysics as onto-theo-logical. I have argued elsewhere, along with many others, that Heidegger was substantially influenced by Luther's critique of Hellenism, and that the roots of his critique of ontotheology are thoroughly Lutheran.[72] Yet Luther nevertheless remained committed to Christianity, and thus his reintroduction of violence into the Godhead never results in a full resurrection of the mythic sacred. However, for Heidegger, the issue remains more obscure, as there indeed occurs a "turn" with regard to his relationship to violence, as the later Heidegger favors an almost radical passivity in his thinking of *Gelassenheit,* despite Heidegger's continued distance from Christianity. Moreover, Heidegger's theological thinking becomes much more sacramental in his later essays. That is, the antireductionism with regard to metaphysics translates for Heidegger to reality as layered with multiple meanings, many of which include the sacred, as it is mediated by human beings and language. In a later essay on Hölderlin entitled "Poetically Man Dwells," Heidegger reflects on the human being as a kind of sacramental *image* of God, where God is imaged forth and made present by way human kindness (*Freundlichkeit*).[73] Heidegger understands this imaging of God by means of human kindness to be ultimately what it means for us to "dwell poetically." Heidegger writes,

> As long as this arrival of kindness endures, so long does man succeed in measuring himself not unhappily against the godhead. When this measuring appropriately comes to light, man creates poetry from the very nature of the poetic.[74]

Thus, for Heidegger poetry is now rethought, no longer as a violent act of techne against the overwhelming forces of nature, but a sacramental imaging of God by way of human kindness, which need not necessarily be "artistic," but simply the disclosure of beauty itself through kindness.

Girard and Heidegger

Girard's major contentions with Heidegger, as we have seen, center on the meaning of Logos, particularly whether the Greek or the Hebraic is the more primordial. Heidegger, at least early in his career, sides with the violent, *polemos*-Logos, whereas Girard sides with the expelled Christian Logos. Nevertheless, Girard lauds Heidegger for disclosing for the first time the fundamental distinction between the two, as other philosophical readings in the Christian tradition had often attempted a sort of syncretism. Indeed, for Girard, the move to the Christian Logos of expulsion represents progress in the history of philosophic thinking, and not regress or "withdrawal" as it does for Heidegger. Thus Girard's "deconstructive" reading of Heidegger in a way mirrors his reading of Nietzsche, in that he praises each thinker for the disclosure of a fundamental insight that remained concealed from everyone else, but disagrees as to the interpretation of this insight.

In Girard's later work on Carl von Clausewitz, *Battling to the End,* Girard discusses yet another fundamental deconstruction of Heidegger, except now by proxy, through the poetry of Hölderlin. We have already hinted at Girard's critique of Heidegger's reading, namely that Heidegger attempted to simply excise all of Hölderlin's Christianity in favor of Hölderlin's Grecophilia." Of particular interest is Girard's understanding of Hölderlin's famous apocalyptic poem "Patmos," which proved to be of decisive importance for Heidegger. The text opens with these famous lines:

> Near is
> And difficult to grasp, God
> But where Danger is, grows
> Salvation also.[75]

Both Girard and Heidegger understand this passage to speak about a withdrawal of the divine. Heidegger famously argued in his essay "The Question Concerning Technology" (1949) that the text indicates a kind of prophesying of the withdrawal of beyng, which at the same time provides a glimmer of hope, namely that human beings could be "drawn along into the withdrawal."[76] That is, for Heidegger, this text speaks of the withdrawal of beyng and thus of the simultaneous flight of the old gods and potential arrival of the new—"only a god can save us." The flight of the gods occurs by way of modern science and technology's reduction of the meaning of being to a singular meaning, thereby crowding out other possible ways "to be," other dimensions to existence, which includes most importantly the sacred dimension. The flight of the gods then represents the danger of the contemporary metaphysical reductionism of the will to power. Yet for Heidegger, it is possible to glimpse the withdrawal of beyng itself in this very danger, *as* this very danger, and thus enact an overcoming; as we have seen, this involves the recognition that beyng itself is involved in its own eclipse. The recognition of this self-eclipse of beyng can occasion the arrival of a new god, a new mythology, by clearing a space for this god to arrive.

Now for Girard, Heidegger's withdrawal of beyng and the gods merely names the positive withdrawal of the violent sacred, and thus, again, Girard differs with Heidegger in interpretation, but not in point of fact. Recall for Girard the "danger" to this withdrawal of the primitive sacred, insofar as this withdrawal leads to the end of the sacrificial system's ability to (violently) contain violence. This cessation of the sacrificial mechanism leads necessarily, by way of the Passion of Jesus, to an *apocalypse,* or to a full disclosure of the system's mechanism, namely the scapegoat. Yet this *apocalypse* can prove "apocalyptic" in that without the mechanism's ability to contain violence and without human being's acceptance of the Kingdom, violence *could* escalate exponentially, even to the point of catastrophic destruction.

However, Girard offers another interpretation to the meaning of Hölderlin's "Patmos" concerning the divine withdrawal, not merely as the withdrawal of the primitive sacred, but the positive withdrawal of Christ that we ourselves are to imitate. Girard writes:

The *presence* of the divine grows as the divine withdraws: it is the withdrawal that saves, not the promiscuity. Hölderlin immediately understood that divine promiscuity can be only catastrophic. God's withdrawal is thus the passage *in Jesus Christ* from reciprocity to relationship, from proximity to distance. . . . Hölderlin thus felt that the Incarnation was the only means

available to humanity to face God's very salubrious silence: Christ ques-
tioned that silence on the cross, and then he himself imitated his Father's
withdrawal by joining him on the morning of his resurrection. . . . We in
turn are thus required to experience *the peril of the absence of God*. . . . To
imitate Christ is to refuse to impose oneself as a model and to always efface
oneself before others. To imitate Christ is to do everything to avoid being
imitated . . . *salvation lies in imitating Christ,* in other words, in imitating
the "withdrawal relationship" that links him with his Father.[77]

Christ imitates the Father's withdrawal he experiences on the cross,
which we in turn are to imitate. Essentially for Girard this means the self-
effacing movement of "dropping out" of the mimetic cycle that we discussed
earlier. It is the movement of nonviolence itself, the willingness to withdraw
from any and every rivalry; it is to refuse to become a model and thus to
refuse to become an obstacle. Thus for Girard this amounts to a move from
reciprocity to relationship, from proximity to distance—that is, from violent
reciprocity to true love of neighbor, from proximity that causes rivalry to
the distance that dissipates it. Girard's reading then amounts to a continual
gestalt shift in understanding the withdrawal of God, at one moment seeing the flight of the violent sacred, and at the next experiencing the true
nonviolent withdrawal of Jesus and imitating that withdrawal in return. It
is a matter of experiencing both meanings simultaneously—of how salvation
grows amid danger, of how God is both near and yet difficult to grasp—for
Christ is always withdrawing. The only way to "grasp" God is to cease trying
to grasp, and rather, as Heidegger advises, let oneself be "drawn along into
the withdrawal."

According to Gianni Vattimo, there remains an indissoluble link that
binds the philosophical "systems"—if one can use that term—of Girard and
Heidegger.[78] This link lies in their hermeneutical unmasking of the violence
that underlies *systems* themselves. Indeed, like the primitive sacred's underlying mimetic mechanism of violent scapegoating, the metaphysical reductionist system, now being promulgated via modern technology, runs on the
underlying violence of mastery and domination of will to power. Thus, for
Vattimo, whether it be will to power in metaphysics or mimetic rivalry in
religion, the desire to reveal and expel the violent contagion remains the
same in both Heidegger and Girard. Indeed Girard helps perfect (or at least

complete) Heidegger, for Vattimo. In the end, Girard shows that it is violence that seeks to reduce the meaning of being to one meaning; it is violence
that seeks to capture being in "objective presence" so as to control it, the very
same violence that sought to expel innocent victims so as to *control* violence.
Vattimo sees both Heidegger's and Girard's theses as that of *weakening* fundamental systems of control and violence. It is by way of these philosophies
of weakness that Vattimo thinks a return to the true mark of Christianity can
take place, namely that of the self-emptying of Christ. It is kenosis then that
best connects the discourses of Girard and Heidegger, which seek to disclose
violence so as to weaken it in order to prepare humans for the fundamental
act of kenosis, whether that be agape or *Gelassenheit*.

CHAPTER 4

A Girardian Critique of Postmodernity

Girard and the Resurrection of Ontotheology

Girard often humbly noted that there is not much that is novel in his mimetic theory, and that Augustine had already voiced the majority of his concerns and insights.[1] Girard's remark is clearly an exaggeration, as his understanding of Judeo-Christianity as a revelation of the scapegoat mechanism is perhaps the most novel idea in twentieth-century philosophy *and* theology. However, Girard and the great doctors of the Church indeed hold much in common, in particular, with regard to their understanding of the scope of "scripture." That is, Aquinas writes in his *Summa Theologiae* in a way that seemingly extends the notion of "scripture" beyond the biblical text itself to include the entire corpus of theology and its axioms, from which further truths can be deduced. So also for Girard the scripture provides the bases from which countless truths (e.g., the truths of mimetic theory) can be inferred and disclosed. The idea that theology is something to be pitted against scripture is a concept that seems to be foreign to Girard, as well as to his Catholic background. As we have seen, it was Luther (and Heidegger following) who introduced the idea that scripture needed to be disentangled from theology, as the latter represents a wholly Greek and thus antibiblical, pagan view of the world. Following Luther, Heidegger's project of the overcoming of metaphysics puts forth an explicit critique of the ontotheological constitution of such metaphysics, which blasphemes God by making God into an object of theoretical speculation. Yet, as I have tried to show, Luther's and Heidegger's critiques of ontotheology and metaphysics remain deeply problematic on several fronts, in particular, the ways in which antiessentialism leads to a resurrection of the mythic and a God "beyond good and evil," as well as the frenzied mimetic rivalry that eventuates from a destruction of the Platonic realm of ideas. And yet Girard remains quite critical of metaphysics, at times, and even lauds deconstructionists like Derrida for their uncovering of hidden mechanisms behind systems. As we saw, it is this disclosive deconstruction, this hermeneutics of suspicion, toward systems' conditions for possibility that makes Girard's thinking so similar to Heidegger's. In other words, Girard, Heidegger, and deconstructionists in general attempt to "think concealment." For Girard, insofar as the Christian tradition attempted to displace a biblical anthropology with that of a Hellenic one, it has erred, since this displacement resulted in a lapsing concealment of the sacrificial mechanism, which can only be revealed by way of the Judeo-Christian Scriptures and their anthropological paradigm of the innocent victim.[2]

Thus Girard's relationship to metaphysics and its ontotheological constitution remains ambiguous in many senses, as his mimetic theory is both laudatory and critical of the Greek thinking, as well as Catholicism's appropriation of it. For Girard, it is Plato who first recognizes the mimetic structure in not only human beings, but in all of reality as well. Indeed, Plato's concerns in the *Republic* (Book II) about the poets largely center upon their use of tragedy and therefore their inscribing of violence into the divine.[3] Plato worried that humans would imitate the gods' own violence and therefore called for an expulsion of the tragic poets in favor of imitation proper, namely philosophical imitation of the true essences of reality, which imitates the one essence itself—Goodness. Eva Brann argues that Plato's real philosophy of aesthetics in the *Republic* is precisely the "philosophical music" of the artists who bypass imitation of the visible world in favor of a direct imitation of the forms themselves, which in turn all image the Good.[4] In other words, Plato expels only those poets who would imitate the finite, visible world and therefore instigate violence and mimetic rivalry, and rather tacitly puts forth a proper *mimetic theory,* namely one that would imitate the divine ideas, the forms, that all image the Good and therefore contain no trace of violence whatsoever. Indeed, Book X of the *Republic* itself concludes with such a philosophical myth that properly imitates the myth of Er, after just having ridiculed the poets for their improper imitation. Plato therefore in a way is forerunner of mimetic theory, as he recognizes the same concerns that Judeo-Christianity recognized, namely the violence inherent in tragedy and therefore the need for human imitation to have recourse to the "other world." Plato thus presents a kind of prototype of the *imitatio Dei* in the character of Socrates; Socrates even is put to death as an innocent victim at the hands of the angry mob of Athens, which Plato's texts knowingly reflect. Thus Platonism and Platonic metaphysics in general have much in common already with the Judeo-Christian tradition; such undoubtedly explains the reasons for the marriage between Athens and Jerusalem that slowly took place from the second century onward.

However, Girard at times chides Plato for his obstinate refusal to recognize mimetic crises among doubles and his choice instead to move the problem of mimesis for artists and poets to bear the full burden.[5] I think Girard is overly critical in his estimation of Plato, for the reasons discussed above, namely Plato's critiques of improper mimesis. Moreover, Girard simply dismisses as anomalous Plato's notion that a just person will almost always ipso facto be punished and killed—even "crucified"—by an angry mob (*Republic* 361b–362a).[6] Yet Girard highlights a fascinating element of Plato's *Republic,* namely its own scapegoating of the poets and its propensity for philosophy itself to devolve into the mythic. That is, Girard views Plato's expelling of the poets as a kind of "Satan casting out Satan," a violence fighting violence.[7] "The Platonic rejection of tragic violence is itself violence, for it finds expression in a new expulsion—that of the poet."[8] It is for this reason that Girard lauds deconstructionists like Heidegger and especially Derrida for their ability to uncover hidden and often times violent elements within Platonism. In particular, Girard on many occasions mentioned with praise Derrida's essay "Plato's Pharmacy," which uncovers Plato's use of the ambiguous *pharmakon,* and the ways in which such use could indicate a violent structure inherent in Platonism itself. "Derrida's analysis demonstrates in striking fashion a certain arbitrary violence of the philosophic process as it occurs in Plato, through the mediation of a word that is indeed appropriate since it really designates an earlier, more brutal variant of the same arbitrary violence."[9] Girard here alludes to the idea that Plato's application of the *pharmakon,* as poison to the Sophists and remedy with regard to Socrates, perhaps indicates a mimetic doubling and thus Plato's unconscious employment of a violent sacrificial term; that is, the word functions for Plato much like the human pharmakos, the scapegoat who is both innocent and guilty simultaneously, which aptly explains Plato's scapegoating of the poets in *Republic.* Thus it seems Girard is willing to concede the Nietzschean-Heideggerian point that Platonism harbors a kind of violence from within, albeit Girard's concession is extremely qualified. Nevertheless, this concession points to, in Girard, a strange relationship with the metaphysical tradition.

However, I think it is clear that Girard is as much of a "Platonist" as any Christian, insofar as he implicitly always affirms the essentialism characteristic of Christian theism, namely in his affirmation of the uniquely "good" and "loving" nature of the Godhead, which in no way concedes to Lutheran voluntarism. God, for Girard, is not "beyond good and evil," but wholly good and nonviolent, and Girard remains quite critical of any attempts to resurrect the *ira Dei* as resurrections of the mythic sacred—for example, Girard's reading of Heidegger.[10] Moreover, and most importantly, it is necessary to preserve the supersensible Platonic realm—the metaphysical realm, as we have seen, for proper mimesis of intelligible reality, lest human beings fall into mimesis of merely the physical world, which, in turn, necessarily eventuates in metaphysical desire. Such was ultimately the tragic fate of Nietzsche's "metaphysics" of the will to power, which, for Girard, inevitably revealed itself to be violence itself.

As noted already, mimetic desire itself is unproblematic, and even essential to human nature; rather it is only a specific type of mimetic desire that leads to mimetic rivalry, namely a desire for the physical and finite, that is, limited resources about which human beings can quarrel and through which they can eventually become obstacles for each other. Proper imitation ought therefore, following Plato, as well as later Christian saints, to be of the immaterial world, where things such as goodness, truth, justice, and so on are plentiful and infinite and do not ipso facto necessitate obstacles and thus violence. For these reasons, then, I think a "Girardian ontology" is simply tantamount to a Platonic one, since proper mimetic desire ought to desire the metaphysical, in short, God. "Good" mimetic desire desires God—and all God's attributes such as goodness, justice, and so on—and seeks to imitate God. In other words, the *imitatio Christi* remains radically inclusive and impervious in a sense from mimetic, metaphysical desire (in the pejorative sense). Such amounts then to Girard's "Platonism," which of course amounts to nothing more than classic Christian theism, as Nietzsche and Heidegger would observe.

As we have seen, Girard's "Platonism" remains at odds with the postmodernism of Nietzsche and Heidegger, insofar as both scapegoat Platonism or simply "metaphysics" itself as the direct cause of violence. For Nietzsche, metaphysics was simply ressentiment and revolt against time qua becoming; for Heidegger metaphysics results in the reduction of being's meaning to univocity. Nietzsche and Heidegger's "postmodernism" then calls for an overcoming and deconstruction of metaphysical, supersensible originals. For Nietzsche and Heidegger, *the* truth is precisely the cause of violence and such truth needs to be left behind. Girard's positions by contrast imply quite the opposite, for it is only belief in immaterial truth that can properly reorient desire from the finite to the infinite. Rather postmodernity remains locked in hypocritical, radical mimesis in its denial of metaphysical reality, since such denial leads to each person competing for originality, which, as we have seen for Girard, results merely in a lust for the novel.

Critique of Postmodernism

Although he undoubtedly perceived the importance of it, Girard has been explicitly critical of postmodern deconstruction insofar as such postmodernism tends toward relativism, in particular the relativism that all being is merely "language" or the "text" without any prime referent.[11] This absence of a prime referent amounts to the same metaphysical problem of anti-Platonism and anti-ontotheology that has become so paramount to postmodernism, namely its critique of the metaphysics of essence, or as Heidegger often puts it, the critique of the metaphysics of "presence." Such critique is nothing more, again, than a critique of Platonism, of metaphysics itself, which seeks to ground the many upon the one, particulars upon universals, and thus, in turn, arrives at the split-world theory of reality: the sensible and the supersensible. Central therefore to this critique is at the same time a critique of reason itself, insofar as it is by way of reason that human beings "know" the intelligible aspects of reality, the one, the universal, the cause, the essence, and so on. It is in this sense that Marxism, Nietzscheanism, and postmodernism all amount to the same critique in that each attempts to posit something more fundamental than reason, namely the nonrational. Whether it is one's economic working conditions, which give rise to ideology, or the will to power that creates values and meanings, it is nevertheless the nonrational that remains concealed behind the rational. Thus Marx, Nietzsche, as well as Heidegger and Derrida, are all suspicious hermeneuts, suspicious of the nonrational, or even irrational, lurking behind the rational. I would like to briefly turn to Nietzsche's hermeneutics of suspicion via his critique of modern science and rationality in order to better prepare an overall, final, Girardian critique of postmodernism and its antiessentialism. As we shall see, regardless of postmodernism's antirationality, antilogic, antiessentialism, and so on, in short, its relativism, it nevertheless remains inextricably bound to Christianity's ethic of concern for victims, which ultimately allows for postmodernism, in the end, to be just another instantiation of Marxism, itself a kind of Christian heresy.

Once again, it is Nietzsche who proves to be the forerunner of this insight into postmodernism. That is, just as Nietzsche, for Girard, gleaned the true essence of Christianity, namely its concern for victims, so too does Nietzsche see that postmodernism is the inevitable consequence of atheistic modern science, which itself cannot cope with its own postmodernism, and thus becomes entrenched ever more in Christianity and its ethic.

In his *The Gay Science* and later in *On the Genealogy of Morals*, Nietzsche notes that Christian theism currently remains alive and well among atheists under the guise of modern science, particularly in modern science's *will to truth*. That is, the atheism of modern science remains nothing of the kind and is thus rather wholly hypocritical insofar as it still not only desires and seeks, but also *values,* the truth, or the idea of a stable, subsisting, intelligible reality that exists behind the phenomenal world. Nietzsche writes,

> Anyone who is truthful in that bold and ultimate sense presupposed by faith in science *thereby affirms a world other* than that of life, nature, and history; and insofar as he affirms this "other world," must he not precisely thereby deny its counterpart, this world, *our* world? . . . It is still a

metaphysical faith on which our faith in science rests—even we knowing ones of today, we godless ones and antimetaphysicians, still also take *our* fire from the flame ignited by a faith thousands of years old, that Christian faith that was also Plato's faith, that God is truth, that truth is divine. . . . Science [therefore] henceforth stands *in need of* justification (which is not to say that it has one[!]).[12]

In other words, atheistic modern science has failed to realize that *if* God is really "dead," then the idea that the human intellect can track an intelligible order to reality—intelligibility itself—remains nothing more than a metaphysical hangover from theism, insofar as theism believed that reality itself was intelligible and rational precisely because it was designed by a Designer. Faith in "truth" (or reason's a capacity to find it) is for Nietzsche tantamount to faith in another world, a meta-physical, supersensible world—the very same world that God occupied in Christianity and thus continues to occupy for science insofar as science still rests upon a metaphysical faith in truth as what "is," over against the phenomenal world of becoming. In short, science represents nothing more than the latest instantiation of what Nietzsche terms the "ascetic ideal," the ideal that would deny this world in favor of a transcendent one. Nietzsche writes, therefore,

These modern-day nay-sayers . . . those who are unconditional on a single point—the claim to intellectual cleanliness—these hard, strict, abstinent, heroic spirits who constitute the honor of our age, all these pale atheists, anti-Christians, immoralists, nihilists, these skeptics, ephetics, hectics of the spirit (for this they are one and all in some sense), these last idealists of knowledge in whom alone intellectual conscience today dwells and is embodied—they in fact believe themselves to be free as possible of the ascetic ideal, these "free, very free spirits" and yet to intimate to them what they themselves cannot see—for they're standing too close to themselves—this ideal is precisely their ideal, too; they themselves represent it, and perhaps no one else; they themselves are its most spiritualized product, its most advanced warriors, and scouts, its most captious, most delicate, most elusive form of seduction—If I am any kind of guesser of riddles, let me try with *this* proposition! . . . they are far from being free spirits, *for they still believe in truth*. (GM 3:24)

It is then, for Nietzsche, the belief in truth, in the *value of truth,* which makes modern science and its "pale atheism," still metaphysical, still ascetic, and thus still Christian.

Thus if science were honest with itself, it would recognize that the purported "death of God" by way of science was simultaneously the "death of Truth" and thus not only the death of God, but the *suicide* of science (qua *scientia*) as well. In other words it would have the courage to at last call into question the very value of truth itself, that is, to perhaps subject the *will to truth* to an immanent critique. Yet atheistic modern science remains largely oblivious to the implications of its deicide. Nietzsche writes,

> Just look at the most ancient and the most recent philosophers: in none
> of them is there any awareness of the extent to which the will to truth
> itself stands in need of justification; there is a gap here in every philoso-
> phy—why is that? Because the ascetic ideal has hitherto *dominated* all of
> philosophy; because truth was posited as being, as God, as the highest
> authority; because truth was simply not *allowed* to be a problem. . . . From
> the moment faith in the god of the acetic ideal is repudiated, *there is a new
> problem as well:* that of the *value* of truth. The will to truth stands in need
> of a critique—here we define our own task—the value of truth must be
> experimentally *called into question.* (GM 3:24)

We could say then that Nietzsche's thinking atheistic modern science through to its essence leads Nietzsche to his own perspectivism, which we would call today his "postmodernism." There are no truths, only perspectives, or, as Nietzsche sometimes puts it, "There are no facts, only interpretations"—even this itself being an interpretation—and "so much the better."[13] As we have seen earlier, Nietzsche sums up his perspective as such: "The world with which we are concerned is false, i.e., is not a fact but a fable . . . it is 'in flux,' as something in a state of becoming, as falsehood always changing but never getting near truth: for—*there is no 'truth'*" (WP 616; emphasis mine).

Yet herein lies the absolute hypocrisy of modern atheism, namely its failure to see this: that, insofar as it still affirms truth, it still remains within the grip of Christianity, of Platonism (which is, after all, "Christianity for the people"). This "theism" of modern science is for the most part still concealed from science. *Modern science remains just as theistic as the theism it thought it had overcome.* What is needed is a recognition of the radical contingency of truth, recognition that "truth" depends upon the fallible human intellect, which if recognized, would result in scientism's transmutation into "postmodernism." Postmodern (perspectivism) therefore liberates "pale atheism" from its Christian stronghold, at least initially, for as we shall see, postmodernism too falls prey to its Christian past and becomes again entrenched in Christianity's absolutism, this time not in terms of Christian metaphysics, but in terms of Christian ethics, and it is here where Girard and Nietzsche meet.

As the pale atheists of modern science transcend their latent Christian faith in truth and embrace the myriad of perspectives that constitutes "postmodernism," they nevertheless, as postmodernists, face another formidable obstacle, a Christian obstacle, and one that remains even more concealed than its predecessor. Postmodernism prides itself on its postrational and post-truth stances and its ability therefore to embrace an infinite number of perspectives and interpretations. However, despite all appearances of postmodernism's being post-Christian, there remains again another indissoluble moral absolute that remains wholly concealed from postmodernism. This moral absolute is, as we have seen (and both Girard and Nietzsche have argued) none other than the *concern for victims.* This concern reigns supreme despite any attempts to case the postmodern moral (and political) landscape as perspectival and pluralistic. Indeed, this absolute value, the concern or compassion for victims, is so self-evident, so axiomatic, and so intuitive that one is hardly even aware that it exists.

Returning again to Nietzsche's critique of slave morality here can prove helpful Essentially, Nietzsche asks us to consider something obvious, so obvious that it is often overlooked: if there is no truth, no being, then what remains is relativism and perspectivism, and if relativism and perspectivism, then morality and even reality simply amounts to power relations (a claim Marxism readily concedes insofar as it understands the world as a history of class conflict); yet if reality is simply about power, will to power, then reality will inevitably bifurcate into those who have power and those who do not. In other words, there will be those who are strong and those who are weak. Now, concerning the strong and weak (or rich and poor, beautiful and ugly, oppressor and oppressed, victimizer and victim, etc.), why should we assume that it is best or virtuous to side with the weak, with the oppressed? Why assume their perspective? Why not assume the strong and powerful perspective? The seemingly innate instinct we have to side with the weak, to feel pity and compassion for the persecuted, for Nietzsche and Girard, is nothing more than the result of two thousand years of habituation—catechesis—in Christianity. That is, Nietzsche (and Girard) asks us to consider why we care for victims, have compassion for weakness, for poverty, and so on? Moreover, as a perspectivalist, Nietzsche asks us to consider whether or not this is simply a perspective, and if so, why assume it is the moral one. For aside from the Judeo-Christian ethic, most if not all prior ethical systems in fact did not side with the weak, but rather with the strong, with the victors. Consider even Aristotelian or Platonic virtues—temperance, courage, magnanimity, and so on, all which seem to indicate strength and mastery over that of weakness—even Latin the word *virtus* itself means essentially "power," and the Greek *aretē* comes from the same root as "aristocratic" or "noble," which indicate superlative superiority (*aristos*).

Yet siding with the weak, victimized, and oppressed is precisely what "we" as a culture, a postmodern culture, do. Again, to even question this moral absolute results in public scorn, for our entire Western morality is based upon it. It seems therefore our postmodern culture is anything but *post*-Christian. Rather it represents an ethic saturated in Christianity, a hyper-Christianity of sorts, where the axiom of concern for victims remains, in a way, the sole moral absolute. This is utterly hypocritical, for Nietzsche, since postmodernity would claim to be "absolutely" perspectival and pluralistic. For why should we assume that this ethic is good? Why ought we to concern ourselves with the defense of victims, the oppressed, the persecuted? There remains, for Nietzsche, ultimately no reason as to why this ethic is enshrined in our culture other than a historically contingent one: we embrace this value simply because we have been trained to do so; that is, our modern attitude of concern for victims represents for Nietzsche two thousand years of catechesis in Judeo-Christianity and its nihilistic asceticism. And if atheists were to be truly honest, they would shrug off this slavish nihilism and consider embracing the Dionysian. In other words, there remains absolutely no reason that we should prefer the Christian ethic to the Dionysian, and thus any honest atheism would reject not only truth, but the Christian ethic as well.

But in fact this is not the case. Postmodernity instead remains oblivious to its own Christian ethic. Moreover it is *obsessed* with victims. One needs only to glance at contemporary American culture and its politics to see its victim obsession. Indeed this obsession is in many ways the fundamental element that structures political discourse. The "Right" and the "Left" are engaged currently in a "battle over victims," a battle over *who* the victim *really* is: is it minorities, members of the LGBTQ community, women (as the Left argues), or is it the white blue-collar worker, the "forgotten man" (as the Right argues)?

Yet in America at least, this ethic is very much a strange, caricatural hyper-Christianity where the ethic of victims has become unhinged from any metaphysical grounding and fused, in a way, with the Dionysian affirmation of violence, insofar as this ethic is now not only an ethic of concern for victims, but also at the same time an ethic of the necessity of persecuting (even violently) victimizers *in the name of victims.* Moreover, there appears to be a kind of collective catharsis felt in publicly shaming and condemning the guilty, those perceived to be *victimizing.* The media consistently parades before us guilty victimizers that are to be judged by the "court of public opinion." Whether it is Harvey Weinstein, Bill Cosby, Bill O'Reilly, there is a certain satisfaction and even pleasure we take in watching these guilty people be judged, condemned, and publicly shamed. Indeed it is cathartic. Notice how it is permissible, in our culture, to judge, condemn, and shame, *so long as* it is done "in the name" of defending victims. Furthermore, there is even, at times, permissiveness toward violence, again, in the name of victims (e.g., the white nationalism that conceives itself as victimized, or members of Antifa who seek to enact violent, public lynchings of fascists in the name of the defense of victims).

Thus, with the rise of "Trumpism"—a term that, I think, includes *both* the Right and the Left—we witness two rather mystifying phenomena: (1) the uprising of persecution (often violent) *in the name of victims,* and (2) simultaneously, in response, the *repudiation* of the concern for victims altogether, whereby "victims" and "the victim mentality" are pejoratives. The latter repudiation of victims, it seems to me, amounts to a neo-Nietzscheanism, a resurrection of fascism and its need to eradicate the weak in the name of power, in the name of making America "great." And yet the former—persecution in the name of victims—confirms Nietzsche's worry about slave ressentiment, namely when violence or persecution is excused in the name of "defending the persecuted."

Postmodernity therefore remains "stuck" in a Christian ethic that it not only cannot see, but thinks it has transcended. Heidegger often remarked that the entire metaphysical tradition from Plato to Nietzsche suffered from the fatal flaw of absolutism and thus of reductionism, both of which remained concealed from metaphysics itself. As we have seen, Nietzsche thought that modern science's atheism was just as theistic as the theism it sought to overcome.[14] Heidegger famously replied that Nietzsche's overcoming of metaphysics was just as metaphysical as the metaphysics it sought to overcome. We can now add to the conversation: postmodernism's overcoming of absolutism is just as absolutist as the absolutism it thinks it has overcome.

Postmodernism therefore contains two essential elements, each of which contradicts the other: (1) a critique, deconstruction, and ultimately destruction of reason, truth, and metaphysics, in short "the death of [the Judeo-Christian] God," and (2) a further entrenchment and affirmation nevertheless in the Judeo-Christian "truth" of ethic of concern for victims. Indeed Heidegger's (if not also Nietzsche's) critique of metaphysics (of truth, rationality, essentialism, etc., as the "metaphysics of presence") is axiomatically assumed by postmodernists such as Derrida, Levinas, and Richard Kearney; moreover, each of these postmodernists also presupposes, particularly Levinas and Kearney (but Derrida as well), the Judeo-Christian ethic under the guises of "difference" and "alterity" that amount to simply a concern or openness toward the "other," in particular, for those who are excluded and marginalized.[15]

Stephen Hicks, in his *Explaining Postmodernism,* has argued that postmodernism, in the end, amounts to a reconfiguration of Marxism, a neo-Marxism, which masquerades under the title of postmodernism but nevertheless interprets reality in terms of the victim ethic, albeit collectively rather than individualistically.[16] That is, insofar as the victim or oppression ethic stands as absolute, and insofar as there remains no metaphysical truth, human history can indeed, as we have already noted, be interpreted collectively in terms of class conflict power relations (e.g., proletariat vs. bourgeoisie). Hicks argues, however, that given the obvious political failings of Marxism in the twentieth century, which include roughly one hundred million deaths under Marxist regimes, Marxism itself could no longer remain a viable political, cultural, or philosophical theory.[17] Instead, Marxism, under the guise of postmodernism, reinterprets the class power relations in light of the victim ethic of oppressor and oppressed, again collectively, but now in terms of a host of collectivist divisions, most prominently race and gender. Regardless, the oppression narrative stands as absolute, as "truth," albeit in collectivist terms, of which Hicks remains highly critical.[18] Hicks views collectivist anti-individualism as the central demon in postmodern neo-Marxism and argues in favor of a return to Enlightenment values that center upon the individual. (It is worth perhaps recalling Nietzsche's observation that individualism itself was a Christian virtue, insofar as the "individual could no longer be sacrificed" in Christianity.)

I largely accept (and, I think, Girard would too) Hicks's reading of the historical rise of postmodernism, as well as the "metaphysical" foundations to postmodernism being tantamount to a kind of Marxism, insofar as it was, in a sense, Marx who inaugurated the hermeneutics of suspicion with regard to reason. Nevertheless, Hicks's interpretation lacks, from a Girardian perspective, as far as I can see, two further elements, namely the necessity of violence inherent in Marxism (and thus postmodernism) and the failure to see that Marxism is a kind of Christianity, or at least founded upon the Judeo-Christian victim ethic. Concerning the latter, Girard (and Nietzsche) rightly point out that "concern for victims" or the "oppression narrative" is Judeo-Christian in origin and not something uniquely innovative to Marxism. It is rather only Marxism's collectivizing of this ethic that proves to be a fundamental distortion. Nevertheless, the ethic itself is Judeo-Christian. Furthermore, perhaps the most well-known words of Karl Marx are that "religion is the opiate of the masses."[19] That is, religion dulls or numbs the necessary rage the victimized ought to feel in their oppression and at their oppressor(s). Rather than spur a revolution by means of the anger wrought by unjust exploitation and oppression, religion teaches the oppressed instead to hope for another world where all injustices will be corrected. In short, for Marxism, religion thwarts revolution, violent revolution, via its suppression of anger and thus violence. It is here that perhaps Marxism most clearly parts with the Judeo-Christian ethic by introducing anger and violence—even "just violence"—into the oppression narrative. Recall, for Girard, Judeo-Christian ethics "works" if and only if it is coupled with nonviolence and "nonresistance" to evil; otherwise, for Girard, victims wind up imitating the evil done unto them by their victimizers and thus fulfill Nietzsche's worry that compassion for the persecuted is nothing more than masked hatred for persecutors. A proper critique of postmodernism qua neo-Marxism must acknowledge, then, both Marxism's debt to the Judeo-Christian ethic and Marxism's problematic assumption that violence can necessarily be coupled with this ethic.

Indeed Girard recognized what he called a "hijacking of the victimary obsession" as a form of neo-Marxism particularly present in the American university.[20] Girard writes,

> As soon as concern for victims is universalized in the abstract and becomes an absolute imperative, it can itself become an instrument of injustice. By a sort of overcompensation, there now exists a tendency to make the mere fact of belonging to a minority group a sort of privilege. Each time purely ethnic and social criteria of selection are substituted for pedagogical talent, for the quality of publications, the American university loses what made it is so effective, namely merit-based competition [i.e., competence]. It's transforming itself into a veritable bureaucracy, a system that's hierarchized according to criteria foreign to successful research or even to effective transmission of knowledge. The fact that this hierarchy inverts this former one doesn't constitute progress. From society's vantage point an upside-down Nietzsche is no better than a right-side-up one who calls for the annihilation of weaklings and losers. . . . In its extreme forms the omnipotence of the victim in our world is becoming such that we may be slipping toward the brink of a new totalitarianism.[21]

Aside from Girard's particular examples here from the American academy, what Girard seems to be alluding to is the preference for the doctrine of "equity," or equality of outcome, over and against that of "equality of opportunity." That is, competence, based upon equal opportunity, is becoming eclipsed in the name of equality of outcome, with preference for perceived victims. Yet Girard's worry seems not necessarily to be about equality of outcome in itself, but rather the means with which such outcomes are put in place or, we could say, instantiated. Thus, what concerns Girard is the potential systemic and bureaucratic totalitarianism that could arise in the name of equality of outcome for victims.

Perhaps then the real problem with Marxism and its later instantiations in postmodernism is quite simply the violence that inevitably ensues insofar as "equity" qua equality of outcome must be enforced from the top down via a techne model of politics whereby the ideal "form" is instantiated into reality. That is, insofar as Marxism and postmodernism embrace equality of outcome over equality of opportunity, and thus seek to manipulate and control representative outcomes (whether equality of class, race, gender, etc.), Marxism must fall prey to a kind of framework (*Gestell*) of controllability noted in Heidegger's critique of technology and science. Such a framework, as we have seen, for Heidegger, is nothing other than the metaphysics of Nietzschean will to power, which, according to Girard is quite simply a metaphysics of violence. In short then, and quite surprisingly, postmodernism qua neo-Marxism must fall under the umbrella of its own critique, in that any equity doctrine leads, or at least could lead, to the violent instantiation of a metaphysical ideal. Again, twentieth-century Marxist history appears to justify this point.

Regardless, postmodern culture, with its various political (neo-Marxist perhaps) configurations, is now a sort of hybrid between the mythic and the Christian, in that it seeks to defend victims while simultaneously victimizing the victimizers. Now, a critique of the logic of the "victimization of victimizers" only works if one accepts the axioms that *all* victims are innocent and that recourse to violence is never helpful in achieving one's ends, namely the defense of victims. Regardless of the correct response to the cultural situation, it remains perhaps more important simply to recognize the occurrence of sacred violence within the postmodern political landscape in the form of its incessant need to condemn publicly guilty victimizers, for condemnation is, I worry, perhaps the only cohesive element left to Western culture.

Postscript

Girard's dialogues with philosopher Gianni Vattimo further highlight Girard's own positions regarding what we have considered under the umbrella term "postmodernism," here vis-à-vis an explicit discussion of relativism (both metaphysical and moral) and nihilism. Vattimo, a formidable philosopher in his own right, considers Girard to be highly influential in helping reconcile his postmodern positions with Christianity. Strangely however, Vattimo writes that "from René Girard I took the idea that God can only be a relativist."[22] For Vattimo, Girard's theories showcase the necessity for privileging Christian love (agape, caritas) above that of "truth" proper.[23] In other words, Christianity cannot be reduced to dogmatic propositions, but rather to social relationships.[24] Thus Vattimo's relativism amounts to something akin to Heidegger's critique of the metaphysics of presence and the reduction of things to a singular meaning.[25] While Girard, throughout his conversations with Vattimo, claims to understand perhaps the practical necessity of identifying as a relativist, he nevertheless remains critical. It is to these criticisms of Vattimo's "relativism" to which we now must turn in order to complete a properly Girardian critique of postmodernism.

The upshot of Girard's critique of Vattimo is quite simply the title of the essay penned by Girard in response to him: "Not Just Interpretations; There Are Facts Too." That is, as noted above, Girard has often made explicit his debt to deconstructive hermeneutics; however, Girard does not allow his affections toward deconstruction to result in a relativism simpliciter. Facts and interpretations are not mutually exclusive. Rather Girard believes there are in fact certain objective truths, among which are the truths of mimetic theory, revealed by Christianity, namely the victim mechanism. Thus, Girard could not in any way maintain a consistent perspectivism (if it is possible for such to be consistently maintained at all), since he indeed believes that one perspective—that of the victim's—is the "true perspective." Mythological perspectives are from the perspective of the crowd, which thinks the victim is guilty; thus, myth distorts the truth and is therefore false. Girard writes, in sum,

> Not only does it [Christianity in Christ's Passion] show us the *truth* that was proper to all previous myths, it makes us see both positions at the same time, one alongside the other. And that, I maintain, is an extraordinary thing. The Passion becomes the key to the understanding of mythology. Myth is always dominated by the viewpoint of the crowd, which designates the victim and proclaims his guilt, whereas in the Passion story we see the other side too, the position of the innocent victim. Now the question is . . . is all of this *true* or *false?* If it is true, we are dealing with an *obvious* self-evident truth. It is principally in these terms that I speak of "truth."[26]

Thus, while Girard respects postmodern, deconstructive strategies at times, including Vattimo's, he would not self-identify as a postmodern *relativist* given the truths of mimetic theory. In other words, for Girard, vis-à-vis the (true) insights of postmodernism, facts and interpretations are not mutually exclusive. Moreover, the problem of self-referential inconsistency, it seems to me, remains an unavoidable and unassailable problem for the relativist, insofar as the position of relativism indeed implicitly still makes a claim to the *truth* that all truths are relative.

This problem of self-referential inconsistency, which we saw earlier with Nietzsche, arises further in Girard's critique of Vattimo regarding Vattimo's positions on morality, especially in light of Vattimo's privileging of caritas over *veritas*. That is, Girard's position is simply again that of Nietzsche's, yet from the opposite side: why should we have concern for victims, for the weak, for the persecuted? Why is this position or perspective "true" over and against all others? In other words, relativism, perspectivism proper, must regard all positions as equal, the very thing Vattimo is of course unwilling to do, and admittedly so. Vattimo, at this point in the dialogue, relents and notes, "My own nihilism [relativism] does not come down to the thesis that there exist no truths."[27] Thus, I assume that Vattimo's qualified relativism amounts to a kind of Heideggerian mistrust of reductionism. However, perhaps "relativism" is no longer the proper term for such a position.

Finally, regarding the question of nihilism (relativism, the rejection of truth) that arises in Vattimo, Girard takes the opportunity to clarify his contention that nihilism itself arises from a misunderstanding of violence:

> With respect to moral nihilism, I would state the following. People think that most of the conflicts today are caused by absolute values, absolute opinions about this or that, what are called "ideologies" or "grand narratives"; they think that absolute opinions generate violence because they generate opposition. There is something aggressive about that, and I think it is a mistaken way of viewing violence in our world and violence in general. Most anthropologists and sociologists still define violence as aggression, but human violence is not aggressive. . . . There is no form of violence in which the actors overtly identity as violent aggressors. [Rather, m]an is essentially competitive and inclined to rivalry. He wants to outdo his neighbor, and so competes with him . . . Nine times out of ten it's not aggressiveness that underlies violence but competition, in which both parties take part.[28]

Nihilism in this context is tantamount to a skepticism regarding abso-lutes, or simply a "mistrust in metanarratives," and is thus synonymous with postmodernism. For Girard, nihilism results from a fundamental error that truth and absolute values are the cause of violence. This fundamental error seems to be in line with not only Arendt's and Heidegger's critique of the techne model of politics, but also Nietzsche's position that "truth" (qua being) itself arises from a resentful attitude toward existence (qua becom-ing). Regardless, Girard thinks that it is not truth that is inherently violent, but rather human beings in their mimetic capacity, which necessarily breeds rivalry. Thus, for Girard postmodern nihilism quite simply misunderstands the nature of human beings, and thus of human violence, and therefore improperly scapegoats truth as the cause of violence, rather than human beings. Postmodernism then is simply another instantiation of mythological scapegoating, where here the myth is simply that there are and can be no truths, since "truth" itself is responsible, guilty even, of all violence.

It is the scapegoating of truth, then, that characterizes our postmod-ern world, a world that scapegoats truth as responsible for violence and thus scapegoats in the name of controlling violence. It is precisely, then, a reconfiguration of the mythic, albeit now attached to the Judeo-Christian ethic, which makes it an unusual caricature, a hyper-Christianity of sorts. For Girard, however, the truth of violence must first be properly understood if culture is ultimately to stabilize violence apart from scapegoating. A proper understanding of violence takes place for Girard only through the revelation of the truths of mimetic theory, which places the heart of human violence within human nature itself, rather than in truth.

Notes

INTRODUCTION

1. For example, Heidegger writes in a later essay entitled "The End of Philosophy and the Task of Thinking" quite straightforwardly, "Throughout the entire history of philosophy, Plato's thinking remains decisive in its sundry forms. Metaphysics is Platonism. [And] Nietzsche characterizes his philosophy as a reverse Platonism." See Martin Heidegger, *Basic Writings* (New York: HarperCollins, 1993), 433.

2. The idea that postmodernism is essentially the French reception of Heidegger has been put forth and well explored by Dominique Janicaud. See *Heidegger in France* (Bloomington: Indiana University Press, 2015). Moreover, Charles Guignon and Derk Pereboom argue that postmodernism is in fact the French reception of Nietzsche such that postmodernism could be perhaps synonymous with "neo-Nietzscheanism." See *Existentialism: Basic Writings,* ed. Charles Guignon and Derk Pereboom (Indianapolis: Hackett Publishing, 2001), 94.

3. Jean-François Lyotard, *The Postmodern Condition* (Minneapolis: University of Minnesota Press, 1984), xxiv.

CHAPTER 1. THE SACRED AS VIOLENCE

1. For a concise summary of Girardian mimetic theory, see Michael Hardin, *Mimetic Theory and Biblical Interpretation* (Eugene, OR: Cascade Books, 2017), 15–31.

2. Many Girard scholars consider there to be a fourth insight, namely Girard's "hominization" thesis, which discusses the role of the victimary mechanism in

the founding of human culture from a Darwinian perspective. However, Girard's discussions of hominization are not quite relevant here for our philosophical purposes and, in my opinion, would simply detract from the metaphysical implications of Girard's first three theses. For a detailed discussion of Girard's theory of hominization, see Chris Haw, "Human Evolution and the Single Victim Mechanism: Locating Girard's Hominization Hypothesis through Literature Survey," *Contagion* 24 (2017): 191–216.

3. In other words, desire (as opposed to need) is initiated by mediators or models. See note 4 below.

4. Girard of course is careful to distinguish between desires and mere needs or appetites, the latter of which are common to everyone regardless of models, and thus depend not on mimesis but on physiology. Hunger, thirst, sexuality, etc., are all basic needs or appetites. However, these needs can become desires once they take on a particular object via mimesis. Thus all humans thirst; however, not all humans desire, e.g., Coca-Cola. For that, it takes a mimetic model.

5. Girard has highlighted this movement from mimetic desire to mimetic rivalry in countless works of literature, in particular the works of Shakespearean tragedy, where one character begins to fall in love with another precisely *because* the person with whom he has fallen in love is *desired* by another. This breeds envy, rivalry, and eventually violence. Moreover, Girard reads Freud's Oedipus complex as illustrating the very heart of mimetic desire and rivalry, albeit mythically. The son's desire for the mother is mediated by the father, who serves as a model for the desire. Thus conflict eventuates between father and son, where the son's desires becomes transmuted as both patricide and incest. For Girard, the Oedipal myth marks only one example, mythically, of mimetic desire leading to mimetic conflict and violence; moreover, Freud reduces the Oedipal situation to a drive, failing to see that the father as model creates the very desire of the son. Therefore, Girard is no Freudian by any stretch. However, Freud does begin to understand, as did many before him, the dangers of mimetic desire, namely rivalry and violence.

6. Girard concludes then that "all desire is [in the end] a desire for being" (René Girard, *When These Things Begin* [East Lansing: Michigan State University Press, 2014], 12). Girard is here strongly influenced by the philosophy of Jean-Paul Sartre, who argued that ultimately *erotic desire* concerns a doomed frustration to try to capture the uncapturable, namely another person's own being, which is, for Sartre, nothingness. That is, I seek in my desire the other's desire, eventually the other's freedom, and finally the other herself. The other and her freedom are for Sartre nothing and thus unable to be possessed. Thus desire—and moreover the human project of existence as a whole—is a mere "useless passion" condemned to inevitable frustration. Such doomed frustration leads eventually, for Sartre, to sadism and masochism, or in other words, *violence*. See Jean-Paul Sartre, *Being and Nothingness* (New York: Washington Square Press, 1956), 471–494, 784.

7. Girard again remains indebted to Sartre, who notably argued that the desire for intersubjectivity led to inevitable frustration, given that human relations are

constituted by a desire to capture the "look" (*la regard*) of another, an ontological impossibility for Sartre that eventuates into either sadism or masochism. Thus, for Sartre, the only semblance of any kind of community of which humans are capable occurs by way of either being subject or object, an "us" or "them," but never both simultaneously. This Sartrean "us vs. them" framework Girard interprets in terms of persecutors and/or persecuted (*When These Things Begin*, 534ff.). See also Jean-Paul Sartre, *Anti-Semite and Jew* (New York: Grove Press, 1962).

8. René Girard, *I See Satan Fall Like Lightning* (Maryknoll, NY: Orbis Books 2001), 70.

9. Girard here follows Freud in arguing that founding murders actually occurred. Freud argued in *Totem and Taboo* and in *Civilization and Its Discontents* that our Oedipal desires originate in an actual death of a father at the hands of his sons. That is, Freud posits that a father once held a harem of women at the expense of his sons, which in turn caused rivalry between the sons and their father and eventuated in the father's murder. Yet due to the sons' subsequent guilt, the father became deified, and ritual reenactment, mythology, and even incest taboos resulted. Such murder and guilt, for Freud, explains why God is most closely associated with father and with conscience and guilt. Moreover, in *Totem and Taboo*, Freud observes that in every tragedy a hero suffers at the hands of the Chorus, which reflects an original mob that directed undiluted wrath against a "guilty" individual. In every tragedy (literally, in Greek, "goat song") for Freud, the "divine goat, Dionysus" is present as the original murdered hero, for tragedy is a reenactment of an original murder of a victim by a mob. Girard finds these original Freudian insights concerning both religion and Greek tragedy immensely important to his overall hypothesis, as we shall see. Most importantly, Girard takes from Freud the hypothesis that an original violence remains the essence of the sacred. See Sigmund Freud, *Totem and Taboo* (New York: Norton, 1950), 192–194.

10. For Girard, again, the "hero" Oedipus serves as a model. In Sophocles's accounts, *Oedipus Rex* and *Oedipus at Colonus*, Thebes suffers from a plague and Oedipus is deemed to be the cause of this plague due to his patricide and incest. Oedipus, as guilty and responsible, is thus the tragic hero made to suffer. In order to end the plague, Oedipus must be banished from the city (*Oedipus at Colonus*) or gouge out his eyes (*Oedipus Rex*). In both cases Girard sees Oedipus's tragedy as his punishment at the hands of the collective mob. Oedipus's divinity lies in his later being revered as a hero who suffered at the hand of fate and whose expulsion and suffering ultimately lead to Thebes's restoration. It is worth noting for Girard that tragedy is a form of myth, except without the violence (i.e., the sacrifice) being visible. Nevertheless the violence done to the hero is certainly implied in his suffering at the hands of fate, at the hands of the Chorus. The tragic too for Girard contains the violent sacred.

11. See, e.g., René Girard, *Evolution and Conversion* (London: Bloomsbury Press, 2008), 83–88. Girard later appears to have slightly modified his position on the linear, historical substituting of animals for human beings. See James Williams, *Girardians* (Hamburg: LIT Verlag, 2013), 204–205.

12. Girard, *When These Things Begin*, 32.

13. Girard, *I See Satan Fall*, 121

14. In the Hebrew prophetic tradition, for example, mercy even begins to trump ritual sacrifice. For example, "I desire mercy, not sacrifice, knowledge of God, rather than burnt offerings" (Hosea 6:6) or "With what shall I come before the LORD . . . shall I come before him with burnt offerings. . . . [Rather the LORD requires you] to do justice, love kindness, and to walk humbly with God" (Micah 6:6–8).

15. Rodney Stark has argued that the virtue of mercy or compassion was largely absent from the ancient world prior to the spread of Christianity. See Rodney Stark, *The Triumph of Christianity* (New York: HarperCollins, 2011), 105–120.

16. Girard, *Evolution and Conversion*, 157.

17. For example, the earlier texts in the Bible, particularly the Pentateuch, contain numerous references to the wrath of Yahweh, which Girard sees as synonymous with the violent sacred (see, e.g., Exodus 4:24–26, Leviticus 26:23–25, 2 Samuel 6:6–7). Moreover, the Yahweh of Exodus indeed asks for animal sacrifice and even instructs Moses on how to offer it (e.g., Exodus 29:19–22, Leviticus 23:19). Nevertheless, there is a progression within the Hebrew Bible and a movement away from animal sacrifice to an ethic of concern for victims. A text like Jeremiah 7:22 even seems to redact the previous commands of Yahweh concerning sacrifice: "For in that day I brought them out of the land of Egypt, I did *not* speak to your fathers or command them concerning burnt offerings and sacrifices" (emphasis mine). Here we see an obvious progression of revelation within the Hebrew Bible, for Jeremiah has Yahweh actually contradict previous passages in the Torah.

18. For example, at the end of the crucifixion, in Luke's account, the Roman centurion, who just participated in the crucifixion himself, exclaims that "truly this was a righteous man," something a mythic persecutor could never do, as he would have been convinced of the victim's guilt (Luke 23:47; see also Matthew 27:54, Mark 15:39). Christ's death is, therefore, as St. Paul calls it, a "spectacle for the world" (Colossians 2:15) that reveals the victim mechanism of all previous mythology.

19. René Girard, *Reading the Bible with René Girard*, ed. Michael Hardin (Lancaster, PA: JDL Press, 2015), 54.

20. Luke 23:24.

21. Girard, *Reading the Bible*, 152.

22. Eventually Raymund Schwager changed Girard's mind to accept the term "sacrifice" in the nonmythic sense. See Girard, *Reading the Bible*, 124–141.

23. Raymund Schwager, *Jesus in the Drama of Salvation* (New York: Crossroad Publishing, 1999), 197.

24. See Matthew 5, Luke 6.

25. See Acts 9:5, 26:15.

26. That is, Girard reads Christ's words here literally (Luke 23:24). Peter's speech at

Pentecost, for Girard, also aligns with the ignorance and therefore, in a sense, innocence, of persecutors (Acts 3:17).

27. Girard, *Reading the Bible*, 118–123.

28. Girard, *Reading the Bible*, 118.

29. See Matthew 12:26, Ephesians 6:12.

30. Girard further notes that, according to Jesus, Satan is "a murderer from the beginning," which Girard interprets to be the original act of the founding murder. See John 8:44.

31. 1 John 2:1, John 14:15–27.

32. Girard, *I See Satan Fall*, 189–190.

33. By showing the Satanic nature in myth, Girard does not wish to imply unequivocally that all archaic religions were merely Satanic, for they were legitimate for their time period at controlling violence and therefore at providing order. The Spirit then also enlightens persecutors in their role as persecutors; the Spirit is therefore the "Spirit of Truth" (John 16:13). See René Girard, *The One by Whom Scandal Comes* (East Lansing: Michigan State University Press, 2014), 55.

34. The pericope of the woman caught in adultery from John's Gospel (John 8) highlights Jesus as the Paraclete, the defender of the victim, even the guilty victim. As the story goes, the collective mob, eager to stone the woman caught "in the very act" (*autophoro*) of cheating on her husband, asks Jesus whether it is just to stone her. Jesus at first avoids their question altogether by writing on the ground, which Girard reads as Jesus's not participating in the mimetic contagion. When pressed, Jesus retorts, "let the one among you without sin cast the first stone." This utterance quickly dissolves the mimetic crisis, as each member of the crowd leaves "one by one" with "their conscience convicted" (John 8:9). Jesus approaches the woman and asks, "where are they who *accuse* [literally, *prosecute*] you? Are there any here who *condemn* [*kata-krinin*]? . . . I do not condemn you either. Go and sin no more." Here Jesus defends even the guilty, the one caught in the very act of sin, from the prosecution and condemnation of the accusers, from *the accuser*.

35. See Matthew 5, Luke 6.

36. See René Girard, *Violence and the Sacred* (Baltimore: Johns Hopkins University Press, 1972), 123. Girard insists, however, that he is not an "unconditional pacifist," since he "does not consider all forms of defense against violence to be illegitimate." Girard, *The One*, 131 n. 3.

37. Girard, *When These Things Begin*, 47; Girard, *Reading the Bible*, 148–149, 160–163; René Girard, *The Girard Reader*, ed. James G. Williams (New York: Crossroad Publishing, 1996), 62–65; Girard, *The One*, 71.

38. Girard, *When These Things Begin*, 47.

39. Girard, *Reading the Bible*, 161.

40. It is for this reason, Girard argues, for example, that Christ emphasizes *the first stone* in

the pericope of the stoning of the adulterous woman in John 8. The first stone is the hardest to throw precisely because there is no one to imitate, that is, there is no model. Once a stone is thrown, mimetic desire will snowball to uncontrollable violence.

41. It is worth noting that the Gospel texts themselves say twice that the *reason* or cause for the death of Jesus was envy (Mark 15:10, Matthew 27:18). This envy is synonymous in John's Gospel to "hating [Jesus] without a cause" (John 15:25)—the very definition of scapegoating, for Girard. That is, there is no reason on the part of Jesus that provokes the violence done to him other than envy. It is often assumed that violence needs to be provoked in order for one to suffer it. However, the New Testament paints quite a different picture. Christ is nonviolent and wholly loving and just, and it is precisely for these reasons that he is envied and eventually murdered. Thus following Christ and choosing to imitate him, in a sense, ipso facto provokes envy and rivalry, which may eventuate in persecution, even violent persecution (John 15:20).

42. Girard, *The Girard Reader*, 65.

43. For example, "As the Father has loved me, so I have loved you. Remain in my love, if you keep my commands you will remain in my love, just as I have kept my Father's commands and remained in his love . . . my command is this: love one another as I have loved you" (John 15:9–11). Here Christ's new commandment of love is grounded upon the imitation of his "remaining" in the Father by imitating the Father's love for Christ, which in turn, is to be imitated by the disciple.

44. Desire for the intelligible *eo ipso* is not always good, as it can indeed be corrupted by mimetic rivalry. However, generally speaking, Girard highlights the "good mimesis" of the saints in their "competition" to outdo each other in goodness, as St. Paul writes (Romans 12:10).

45. Lyotard, *The Postmodern Condition*, xxiv.

46. See Hannah Arendt, *The Human Condition* (Chicago: University of Chicago Press, 1958), 220–230; also Hannah Arendt, "Thinking and Moral Consideration," *Social Research* 38, no. 3 (1971): 417–446.

47. Arendt, *The Human Condition*, 224–225.

48. Arendt, "Thinking and Moral Consideration," 435ff.

49. Heidegger, *Basic Writings*, 260.

50. René Girard, "Innovation and Repetition," *Substance* 19, nos. 2–3, issue 62–63 (special issue: Thought and Novation, 1990): 7–20.

51. Ibid.

CHAPTER 2. NIETZSCHE'S RELIGIOUS HERMENEUTICS

1. Girard, *The One*, 35.

2. Friedrich Nietzsche, *Beyond Good and Evil* (New York: Penguin, 1995), preface.

3. Girard's essay "Nietzsche versus the Crucified" is also quite thorough and novel in its treatment of Nietzsche; however, this chapter from *I See Satan Fall Like Lightning* is, in a way, more developed, as it comes later in Girard's career and thus Girard has had more time to ruminate over Nietzsche's fundamental insights that were nevertheless first identified in his earlier essay.

4. Girard, *I See Satan Fall*, 171.

5. Friedrich Nietzsche, *The Will to Power* (New York: Vintage Press, 1968), para. 1052. Further textual references will be indicated by WP and paragraph number.

6. Girard, *The Girard Reader*, 247.

7. Friedrich Nietzsche, *On the Genealogy of Morals* (New York: Vintage Press, 1989), 119. Further textual references will be indicated by GM and chapter and paragraph number.

8. Nietzsche chooses the French *ressentiment* over the German *Rache* likely due to *ressentiment*'s etymological significance as a repetition of a "sentiment" or feeling.

9. Girard, *I See Satan Fall*, 173.

10. Girard, *The Girard Reader*, 250.

11. Ibid.

12. Friedrich Nietzsche, *The Twilight of the Idols and The Anti-Christ* (New York: Penguin, 1990), para. 2. Further textual references to *The Anti-Christ* will be indicated by A and paragraph number.

13. Friedrich Nietzsche, *The Birth of Tragedy* (New York: Vintage Press, 1967), sec. 1.

14. Ibid., 7.

15. For Girard's detailed reflections on the antisacrificial notion of the atonement, see René Girard, *Things Hidden since the Foundation of the World* (Stanford: Stanford University Press, 1987), 180–223.

16. René Girard, *To Double Business Bound* (Baltimore: Johns Hopkins University Press, 1988), 74.

17. Ibid.

18. Martin Heidegger, *Nietzsche*, vol. 3: *The Will to Power as Knowledge and as Metaphysics*, ed. David Farrell Krell (New York: Harper & Row, 1987), 170, 189; see Martin Heidegger, *The Question Concerning Technology and Other Essays*, trans. William Lovitt (New York: Harper & Row, 1977), 82.

19. Heidegger, *Nietzsche*, 3:195.

20. Ibid., 3:197.

21. Martin Heidegger, *Nietzsche*, vol. 4: *Nihilism* (New York: Harper & Row, 1982), 7.

22. Girard, *When These Things Begin*, 69.

23. Ibid., 135.

24. Girard, *To Double Business Bound*, 76.

25. Heidegger writes, e.g., "Metaphysics is Platonism." Martin Heidegger, *On Time and Being* (Chicago: University of Chicago Press, 2002), 57.

26. For example, Nietzsche writes, "In ages of crude, primordial cultures, man thought he could come to know a second real world in dreams: this is the origin of all metaphysics. Without dreams man would have found no occasion to divide the world." Friedrich Nietzsche, *Human, All Too Human* (Lincoln: University of Nebraska Press, 1986), 16. See also Nietzsche's brief history of Platonism/metaphysics in "On How the 'Real World' at Last Became a Myth" (*Twilight of the Idols*, 50). I will return to specific connections between dividing the world, Platonism, and science in Nietzsche's *On the Genealogy of Morality* in chapter 4.

27. Friedrich Nietzsche, *Thus Spoke Zarathustra*, trans. Walter Kaufmann (New York: Modern Library, 1995), chap. 2, sec. 20.

28. The equating of metaphysics with theology, at least natural theology, first arises in Aristotle (*Metaphysics* 1026a, 1072a–b).

29. Martin Heidegger, *What Is Called Thinking?* (New York: Harper and Row, 1968), 85.

30. Nietzsche, *Thus Spoke Zarathustra*, chap. 2, sec. 7.

31. Martin Heidegger, *Nietzsche*, vol. 2: *The Eternal Recurrence of the Same* (New York: Harper & Row, 1984), 221; Heidegger, *What Is Called Thinking*, 98.

32. Girard, *The One*, 7.

33. Ibid.; Girard, *Evolution and Conversion*, 34.

34. Girard, *I See Satan Fall*, 175.

35. Ibid., 175–176.

36. Ibid., 177.

37. Ibid., 179.

CHAPTER 3. HEIDEGGER'S VIOLENT SACRED

1. Girard, *Things Hidden*, 265.

2. See Martin Heidegger, *Early Greek Thinking* (San Francisco: Harper San Francisco, 1985), 71.

3. Girard, *Things Hidden*, 267.

4. John Sallis, *Being and Logos* (Bloomington: Indiana University Press, 1996), 1–22.

5. Martin Heidegger, *Introduction to Metaphysics* (New Haven: Yale University Press, 2000), 65.

6. Ibid.

7. Ibid., 154.

8. Ibid., 111.

9. Ibid., 112.

10. Girard, *Things Hidden*, 271.

11. René Girard, *Sacrifice* (East Lansing: Michigan State University Press, 2011), 85.

12. Girard, *Things Hidden*, 276.

13. It is worth noting that Nietzsche scholarship has drawn a parallel between Nietzschean ontology and Heraclitus. Indeed, Matthew Meyer argues that Nietzsche's "metaphysics" is quite simply Heraclitean. See Matthew Meyer, *Reading Nietzsche through the Ancients* (Berlin: De Gruyter, 2014).

14. Martin Heidegger, *Identity and Difference* (New York: Harper & Row, 1969), 72.

15. Heidegger, *Early Greek Thinking*, 71.

16. Ibid.

17. Ibid., 72.

18. Martin Heidegger, *Parmenides* (Bloomington: Indiana University Press, 1998), 104.

19. Heidegger, *Early Greek Thinking*, 74.

20. Heidegger, *Basic Writings*, 162.

21. Ibid., 180.

22. Ibid., 198; emphasis mine.

23. Martin Heidegger, *The Heidegger Reader* (Bloomington: Indiana University Press, 2009), 145.

24. Heidegger, *Basic Writings*, 168.

25. Ibid., 169.

26. Ibid., 174.

27. Heidegger, *Introduction to Metaphysics*, 160.

28. Ibid., 161.

29. Ibid.; emphasis mine.

30. Ibid., 171.

31. Ibid., 176.

32. Martin Heidegger, *Elucidations on Hölderlin's Poetry* (New York: Humanity Books, 2000), 52.

33. Ibid., 65.

34. Ibid., 57.

35. Ibid., 61.

36. Ibid., 60.

37. Ibid., 62.

38. Ibid.

39. Ibid., 64.

40. Ibid., 76.

41. Heidegger, *The Heidegger Reader*, 160.

42. Ibid., 172–173.

43. See William Richardson, *Through Phenomenology to Thought* (The Hague: Martinus Nijhoff, 1974), 430–431.

44. Heidegger, *Elucidations on Hölderlin's Poetry*, 97–98. "Das Heilige 'älter denn die Zeiten' und 'über die Götter' gründet in seinem Kommen einen anderen Anfang einer anderen Geschichte. Das Heilige entscheidet anfänglich zuvor über die Menschen und über die Götter, ob sie sind und wer sie sind und wie sie sind und wann sie sind. Kommendes wird in seinem Kommen gesagt durch das Rufen. Hölderlins Wort ist jetzt, mit diesem Gedicht anhebend, das rufende Wort.... Das Heilige verschenkt das Wort und kommt selbst in dieses Wort. Das Wort ist das Ereignis des Heiligen. Hölderlins Dichtung ist jetzt anfängliches Rufen, das vom Kommenden selbst gerufen, dieses und nur dieses das Heilige sagt. Das hymnische Wort ist 'heiliggenöthiget.'" Martin Heidegger, *Gesamtausgabe*, vol. 4: *Erläuterungen zu Hölderlin's Dichtung* (Frankfurt am Main: Vittorio Klostermann, 1981), 76–77.

45. Karen Gover expounds on and details, as much as is possible, Heidegger's notion of the tragic, especially with regard to *Besinnung* and his pre-Socratic fragments. Her conclusion, as I understand it, is that Heidegger himself remains uncertain and unclear as to precisely how the tragic fits within his own thinking, especially the critique of metaphysics. According to Gover, Heidegger both "distances" and "embraces" the tragic as a characterization of his own philosophy. Nevertheless, it seems Heidegger certainly sought to find a place for the tragic within his own thinking; whether or not he found it is another matter. See Karen Gover, "Tragedy and Metaphysics in Heidegger's 'The Anaximander Fragment,'" *Journal of the British Society for Phenomenology* 40, no. 1 (2009): 37–53.

46. Martin Heidegger, *Mindfulness* (London: Continuum, 2006), 197.

47. "Die Frage: Was ist Metaphysik?, im Bereich des Übergangs zum anderen Anfang gestellt ..., erfragt das Wesen der 'Metaphysik' bereits im Sinne einer ersten Gewinnung der Vorfeldstellung zum Übergang in den anderen Anfang. Mit anderen Worten, sie fragt schon aus diesem her. Was sie als Bestimmung der 'Metaphysik' sichtbar macht, das ist schon nicht mehr die Metaphysik, sondern ihre Überwindung." Martin Heidegger, *Gesamtausgabe*, vol. 65: *Beiträge zur Philosophie: Vom Ereignis* (Frankfurt am Main: Vittorio Klostermann, 1989), 171–172 (translation mine).

48. Heidegger, *Basic Writings*, 329.

49. Martin Heidegger, *Contributions to Philosophy: From Enowning* (Bloomington: Indiana University Press, 1995), 283.

50. Girard, *The Girard Reader*, 283.

51. John D. Caputo, *Demythologizing Heidegger* (Bloomington: Indiana University Press, 1993), 177–179.

52. See Duane Armitage, *Heidegger's Pauline and Lutheran Roots* (New York: Palgrave Macmillan, 2016), 93–102.

53. Clare Pearson Geiman, "Heidegger's Antigones," in *A Companion to Heidegger's "Introduction to Metaphysics,"* ed. Richard Polt and Gregory Fried (New Haven: Yale University Press, 2001), 161–182.

54. Ibid., 312.

55. Richardson, *Through Phenomenology to Thought*, 209ff.

56. Ibid., 519 n. 11.

57. See Gil Bailie, *Violence Unveiled* (New York: Crossroad Publishing, 1995), 254–259.

58. See Heidegger, *Mindfulness*, 209–212.

59. Ibid. See also Martin Heidegger, *Basic Problems of Phenomenology* (Bloomington: Indiana University Press, 1988), 81–87, 104–105.

60. See Armitage, *Heidegger's Roots*, 86–87.

61. See ibid., 18–20.

62. Martin Luther, *Lectures on Romans* (Philadelphia: Westminster Press, 1961), 236–237.

63. Ibid., 29.

64. Ibid., 18.

65. Luther even famously adds the world "alone" (*allein*) to his German translation of Romans 3:28.

66. Martin Luther, *Early Theological Works* (Philadelphia: Westminster Press, 1962), 269–270.

67. Martin Luther, *Selections* (New York: Anchor Books, 1964), 190–192.

68. See, for example, Luther's glosses on Romans 8:28 in *Lectures on Romans*, 246–259.

69. Ibid., 29.

70. Heidegger, *Basic Writings*, 260.

71. See Richard Kearney, *The God Who May Be* (Bloomington: Indiana University Press, 2001), 1; John D. Caputo, *The Weakness of God* (Bloomington: Indiana University Press, 2006), 7–15.

72. See Armitage, *Heidegger's Roots*, 13–32.

73. Martin Heidegger, *Poetry, Language, Thought*, trans. Albert Hofstadter (New York: Harper & Row, 1971), 223.

74. Ibid., 227.

75. Nah ist
Und schwer zu fassen der Gott.
Wo aber Gefahr ist, wächst
Das Rettende auch.

76. Heidegger, *What Is Called Thinking*, 18.

77. René Girard, *Battling to the End* (East Lansing: Michigan State University Press, 2009), 122–123.

78. René Girard and Gianni Vattimo, *Christianity, Truth, and Weakening Faith*, ed. Pierpaolo Antonello (New York: Columbia University Press, 2010), 78–87.

CHAPTER 4. A GIRARDIAN CRITIQUE OF POSTMODERNITY

1. Girard, *When These Things Begin*, 133.

2. Ibid.

3. See Girard, *The One*, 120.

4. Eva Brann, *The Music of Plato's Republic* (Philadelphia: Paul Dry Books, 2011), 153, 170–172.

5. Girard, *Evolution and Conversion*, 43; Girard, *The One*, 6; Girard, *When These Things Begin*, 12.

6. Girard, *Evolution and Conversion*, 49.

7. Girard, *Violence and the Sacred*, 295–296.

8. Ibid., 295.

9. Ibid., 296.

10. See Girard, *The Girard Reader*, 276.

11. Girard, *Reading the Bible*, 58–59.

12. Friedrich Nietzsche, *The Gay Science*, trans. Walter Kaufmann (New York: Vintage, 1974), sec. 344.

13. Nietzsche, *Beyond Good and Evil*, 22.

14. For this particular "reductionistic" interpretation of Heidegger's critique of metaphysics, see Duane Armitage, *Heidegger and the Death of God: From Plato to Nietzsche* (New York: Palgrave Pivot, 2017).

15. Kearney's, Derrida's, and Levinas's works are littered with continual references to these axioms. Perhaps the most clear and concise formulation and admission to precisely these two specific axioms, by all three thinkers, can be found in a set of conversations organized by Richard Kearney. Kearney and Levinas appear to be self-aware of their appropriation of this ethic. See Richard Kearney, *Debates in Continental Philosophy: Conversations with Contemporary Thinkers* (New York: Fordham University Press, 2004), 73–77, 154–155, 253–260.

16. Stephen Hicks, *Explaining Postmodernism* (Roscoe, IL: Ockham's Razor Publishing 2011), 1–20, 135–170. Hicks's thesis, in a sense, is hardly controversial in that most philosophers considered to be "postmodern" openly acknowledge Marxism, or at least some debt to Marx. Hicks has done an impressive job in detailing postmodern philosophers' explicit commitments to Marxism.

17. "Postmodernism is the academic far Left's epistemological strategy for responding to the crisis caused by the failures of socialism in theory and in practice" (ibid., 89).

18. Hicks is not alone in acknowledging Postmodernism's necessary connection to Marxism and, in particular, the "victim ethic." For example, Christopher Butler has argued that the single most important postmodern ethical argument concerns discourses of power, and subsequently who by way of those discourses are marginalized and excluded. See Christopher Butler, *Postmodernism: A Very Short Introduction* (Oxford: Oxford University Press, 2002), 44ff.

19. Karl Marx, *A Contribution to a Critique of Hegel's Philosophy of Right*, from https://www.marxists.org/archive/marx/works/1843/critique-hpr/intro.htm.

20. Girard, *When These Things Begin*, 37.

21. Ibid., 38.

22. Vattimo and Girard, *Christianity, Truth*, 48.

23. Ibid., 48–52.

24. Ibid., 52.

25. Whether or not this position should be conflated with relativism is not quite my concern here, since Vattimo simply asserts relativism and argues that Girard's insights ought to lead to such relativism. However, I am inclined to disagree, and Girard will as well.

26. Vattimo and Girard, *Christianity, Truth*, 43.

27. Ibid., 61.

28. Ibid., 59–60.

Bibliography

Arendt, Hannah. *The Human Condition*. Chicago: University of Chicago Press, 1958.

———. "Thinking and Moral Consideration." *Social Research* 38, no. 3 (1971): 417–446.

Armitage, Duane. *Heidegger and the Death of God: From Plato to Nietzsche*. New York: Palgrave Pivot, 2017.

———. *Heidegger's Pauline and Lutheran Roots*. New York: Palgrave-Macmillan, 2016.

Bailie, Gil. *Violence Unveiled*. New York: Crossroad Publishing, 1995.

Brann, Eva. *The Music of Plato's Republic*. Philadelphia: Paul Dry Books, 2011.

Butler, Christopher. *Postmodernism: A Very Short Introduction*. Oxford: Oxford University Press, 2002.

Caputo, John D. *Demythologizing Heidegger*. Bloomington: Indiana University Press, 1993.

———. *The Weakness of God*. Bloomington: Indiana University Press, 2006.

Freud, Sigmund. *Totem and Taboo*. New York: Norton & Co., 1950.

Geiman, Clare Pearson. "Heidegger's *Antigones*." In *A Companion to Heidegger's Introduction to Metaphysics,* edited by Richard Polt and Gregory Fried. New Haven: Yale University Press, 2001.

Girard, René. *Battling to the End*. East Lansing: Michigan State University Press, 2009.

———. *Evolution and Conversion*. London: Bloomsbury Press, 2008.

———. *The Girard Reader*. Edited by James G. Williams. New York: Crossroad Publishing, 1996.

———. *I See Satan Fall Like Lightning*. Maryknoll, NY: Orbis Books, 2001.

———. "Innovation and Repetition." *Substance* 19, nos. 2–3, issue 62–63 (special issue: Thought and Novation, 1990): 7–20.

———. *The One by Whom Scandal Comes*. East Lansing: Michigan State University Press, 2014.

———. *Reading the Bible with René Girard*. Edited by Michael Hardin. Lancaster, PA: JDL Press, 2015.

———. *Sacrifice*. East Lansing: Michigan State University Press, 2011.

———. *Things Hidden since the Foundation of the World*. Stanford: Stanford University Press, 1987.

———. *To Double Business Bound*. Baltimore: Johns Hopkins University Press, 1988.

———. *Violence and the Sacred*. Baltimore: Johns Hopkins University Press, 1972.

———. *When These Things Begin*. East Lansing: Michigan State University Press, 2014.

Girard, René, and Gianni Vattimo. *Christianity, Truth, and Weakening Faith*. Edited by Pierpaolo Antonello. New York: Columbia University Press, 2010.

Glover, Karen. "Tragedy and Metaphysics in Heidegger's 'The Anaximander Fragment.'" *Journal of the British Society for Phenomenology* 40, no. 1 (2009): 37–53.

Hardin, Michael. *Mimetic Theory and Biblical Interpretation*. Eugene, OR: Cascade Books, 2017.

Haw, Christopher. "Human Evolution and the Single Victim Mechanism: Locating Girard's Hominization Hypothesis through Literature Survey." *Contagion* 24 (2017): 191–216.

Heidegger, Martin. *Basic Problems of Phenomenology*. Bloomington: Indiana University Press, 1988.

———. *Basic Writings*. New York: HarperCollins, 1993.

———. *Contributions to Philosophy: From Enowning*. Bloomington: Indiana University Press, 1995.

———. *Early Greek Thinking*. San Francisco: Harper San Francisco, 1985.

———. *Elucidations on Hölderlin's Poetry*. New York: Humanity Books, 2000.

———. *Gesamtausgabe*, vol. 4: *Erläuterungen zu Hölderlin's Dichtung*. Frankfurt am Main: Vittorio Klostermann, 1981.

———. *Gesamtausgabe*, vol. 65: *Beiträge zur Philosophie: Vom Ereignis*. Frankfurt am Main: Vittorio Klostermann, 1989.

———. *The Heidegger Reader*. Bloomington: Indiana University Press, 2009.

———. *Identity and Difference*. New York: Harper and Row, 1969.

———. *Introduction to Metaphysics*. New Haven: Yale University Press, 2000.

———. *Mindfulness*. London: Continuum, 2006.

———. *Nietzsche,* vol. 2: *The Eternal Recurrence of the Same*. New York: Harper & Row, 1984.

———. *Nietzsche,* vol. 3: *The Will to Power as Knowledge and as Metaphysics*. Edited by David Farrell Krell. New York: Harper & Row, 1987.

———. *Nietzsche,* vol. 4: *Nihilism*. New York: Harper & Row, 1982.

———. *On Time and Being*. Chicago: University of Chicago Press, 2002.

———. *Parmenides*. Bloomington: Indiana University Press, 1998.

———. *Poetry, Language, Thought*. New York: Harper & Row, 1971.

———. *The Question Concerning Technology and Other Essays*. Translated by William Lovitt. New York: Harper & Row, 1977.

———. *What Is Called Thinking*. New York: Harper & Row, 1968.

Hicks, Stephen. *Explaining Postmodernism*. Roscoe, IL: Ockham's Razor Publishing, 2011.

Janicaud, Dominique. *Heidegger in France*. Bloomington: Indiana University Press, 2015.

Kearney, Richard. D*ebates in Continental Philosophy: Conversations with Contemporary Thinkers*. New York: Fordham University Press, 2004.

———. *The God Who May Be*. Bloomington: Indiana University Press, 2001.

Luther, Martin. *Early Theological Works*. Philadelphia: Westminster Press, 1962.

———. *Lectures on Romans*. Philadelphia: Westminster Press, 1961.

———. *Selections*. New York: Anchor Books, 1964.

Lyotard, Jean-François. *The Postmodern Condition*. Minneapolis: University of Minnesota Press, 1984.

Marx, Karl. *A Contribution to a Critique of Hegel's Philosophy of Right*. From https://www.marxists.org/archive/marx/works/1843/critique-hpr/intro.htm.

Meyer, Matthew. *Reading Nietzsche through the Ancients*. Berlin: De Gruyter, 2014.

Nietzsche, Friedrich. *The Birth of Tragedy*. New York: Vintage Press, 1967.

———. *Beyond Good and Evil*. New York: Penguin, 1995.

———. *The Gay Science*. New York: Vintage Press, 1974.

———. *Human, All Too Human*. Lincoln: University of Nebraska Press, 1986.

———. *On the Genealogy of Morals*. New York: Vintage Press, 1989.

———. *Thus Spoke Zarathustra*. Translated by Walter Kaufmann. New York: Modern Library, 1995.

———. *The Twilight of the Idols and The Anti-Christ*. New York: Penguin, 1990.

———. *The Will to Power*. New York: Vintage Press, 1968.

Richardson, William. *Through Phenomenology to Thought*. The Hague: Martinus Nijhoff, 1974.

Sallis, John. *Being and Logos*. Bloomington: Indiana University Press, 1996.

Sartre, Jean-Paul. *Anti-Semite and Jew*. New York: Grove Press, 1962.

———. *Being and Nothingness*. New York: Washington Square Press, 1956.

Schwager, Raymund. *Jesus in the Drama of Salvation*. New York: Crossroad Publishing, 1999.

Stark, Rodney. *The Triumph of Christianity*. New York: HarperCollins, 2011.

Williams, James G. *Girardians*. Hamburg: LIT Verlag, 2013.

Index

and concern for victims, 15, 39, 101; and Continental philosophy, 2; as critical of Christ's death as sacrifice, 7; critiques by, 14; essential insights of, 2, 18, 51, 54, 85, 88, 94; on Dasein, 37; and death of God, 13; and *diabolos*, 8, 28; and Dionysian *mania*, 33; essential theses of, 1, 2, 88, 108n2; on *the first stone*, 111n40; follows Freud's Oedipal thought, 109n9; on fourth "hominization" insight, 107–8n2 (chap. 1); on Greek philosophy as abstraction, 51; "hegemony of reason" reframed, xiv; hermeneutic of, 51; on Hölderlin, 85, 86–87, 118n75; on "holy," 6; and ignorance as innocence, 111n26; innovation and creativity, 12; "Innovation and Repetition," 12; inverts master and slave, 28; *I See Satan Fall Like Lightning*, 113n3; on Jesus Christ's passion, 6, 39; on Logos, philosophy of, 51–53, 85; on myth as Satanic, 9; on mythic god, 27; and mythic sacred resurrection, 92; on National Socialism, 16; Oedipus complex models of, 3, 5, 108n5, 109nn9–10; "other" as model of, 2; on paganism, 26; and *Paracletos* as legal metaphor, 8; and persecution, 39; rationality and critique of reason by, xiv; on religion as release, 3; on resentment, 28; on sacred, 4, 42, 109n9; and sacrifice, 2, 110n22; and Satan as accuser, 8; and Vattimo, 104; on victimization, 4, 6, 8–9, 105; and violence from within, 92. *See also* mimetic desire; mimetic rivalry; mimetic theory; mimetic violence; ontotheology

Girard on Heidegger, xiv, 2, 11, 14, 84; and beyng compared to sacred, 77; and beyng's poetic founding, 70; circling primitive sacred, 65; deconstructive reading of, 85, 91; disagrees with Logos interpretation, 41–42; and Christian

Logos, 41, 54, 85; Christianity insights of, 41; and Greek Logos, 41, 42, 51, 54, 85; and Hebraic Logos, 41, 51, 54, 85; on Heraclitean Logos, 52, 54; and insight on Logos, 51, 52; on metaphysics, as ontotheology, 42; on metaphysics overcome by Logos, 51; on metaphysics priority over ethics, 38; on myth restored, 51, 70; and myth and ritual, 65; and mythic sacred, 92; on Nietzscheanism and Nazism, 38; and philosophy bound to Heidegger, 87, 88; and praise, 85; as religious thinker on violent sacred, 41, 42, 51, 72; and violence, 52, 54

Girard on Judeo-Christianity: and desacralization, 6; and following Christ provokes envy and rivalry, 29, 112n41; on Gospel of John, 55–56; and mythic sacred, x, xiv, 1, 53, 55, 66, 71, 77, 84, 92; and non-violence, 101; and religion as cathartic release, 3; as revelation of scapegoating mechanism, 89; on satanic nature of myth, 111n33; on scapegoating of Jesus, 5, 7; and theology versus scripture, 89; and tragedy as form of myth, 109n10; and understanding scope of "scripture," 89

Girard on Nietzsche, 2, 11, 14, 17, 20; agreeing on resentment-fueled "Christianity," 39; and anti-Christianity, 38; and failure to overcome Platonism, 37; and ideology of mimetic desire, 37; and metaphysics of violence, 37; on Nietzscheanism and Nazism, 38; on Nietzschean morality, 18, 21–29; on Nietzschean will to power as violence, 28–33; Nietzsche praised by, 15, 16, 21; on "Nietzsche versus the Crucified" essay, 19, 33, 113n3; on Nietzsche's critique of metaphysics, 33; on Nietzsche's desire for complete originality, 37; on Nietzsche's madness, 33; on Nietzsche's only error, 33; on Nietzsche's sole

flaw, 100; on *a-letheia*, 44; on *aletheia*, 4, 46, 49, 59–60, 62, 68–69, 73–74; ambiguity of writings by, 68, 73; on *Antigone*, 67, 78; Aristotle followed by, 61–62; and art work as cultural thought and mimesis, 61–65, 68, 69; "As When on a Holiday" essay by, 71, 72; and "authenticity," 37; on banality of evil, 12; *Basic Problems of Phenomenology*, 80; *Beiträge*, 66, 75; *Besinnung*, 75, 116n45; changes in thinking of, 77, 78; on Christian thinking, 77; Christianity critiqued by, xi, 77, 79; on "clearing," 46, 63, 72, 83; and concealment, 49–50, 63, 83; Continental philosophy dominated by, x; *Contributions to Philosophy*, 50, 74–75; critique on technology and science, 103; critiqued by Girard, 86; and Dasein, 44, 47–48, 68, 75, 80; and deconstruction, 44, 59, 85; and *deinon*, 67, 78; differs from early Christian philosophy, 54; and *dikē* or justice, 68; and divine, 61, 69, 85; on earth and world in struggle, 62, 63, 64; "The End of Philosophy and the Task of Thinking," 107n1 (Intro.); and *Ereignis*, 46; and Eternal Return, 29; on evil, 83; on *ex-listere*, 48; on flight of the gods, 86; on founding of worlds, 66, 68; on *Gestell*, 48–49, 78–79, 103; and God as being, 58, 59; on god's space, 64; and to "grasp" God, 87; on grounding, 58; and *der Grund*, 43, 44; on *Hen-Panta*, 59–61, 64, 69; on Heraclitus's fragments, 60, 66; on history as tragic fate, 76; "Hölderlin and the Essence of Poetry," 69; on Hölderlin's poetry, 66, 69–76, 84, 116n44; and the holy, 64, 65–66, 71–75, 77, 79; on human kindness, 84; influences on, xi; and *Kehre*, as away from violence, 77, 78; on language and Logos, 69; and *legein*, 59; "Letter on Humanism," 83; and Logos's dual

nature, 69; "Logos" essay by, 59, 61; on Logos/Logos as one, 41, 59, 60–61, 66, 69; on Logos and *polemos*, 54, 61, 63, 66, 68, 72; Luther influenced, 84; on myth (sage), 64; on mythic sacred resurrection, 71; on naming, 63, 69, 74, 76; on Nietzsche, xi, 29, 34, 78, 100; Nietzschean will to power, 49; and Nietzsche lectures, 78; on and notion of the tragic, 116n45; on *Oedipus Rex*, 54; ontotheological critique by, 79; and ontotheology, overcoming, 59; "The Origin of the Work of Art," 61; "Patmos," importance to, 85, 86; and perspectivism, 49; phenomenology of, xi; on philosophy as bound to Girard, 87, 88; and Plato, 58, 107n1 (Intro.); on *phusis* (nature), 7, 72, 73; "Poetically Man Dwells," 84; and *polemos*, 60, 61, 63, 64–68, 72, 77–78; "The Question Concerning Technology," 85–86; and *ratio*, 59, 80; and reality demythologized, 51; and reason wedded to truth, xvi; reflexive mimesis of, 62, 63; as religious thinker, 41, 58; on revenge, overcoming, 34–35; on sacrifice, 65; and Sophocles, 67; and techne, 12, 68, 74, 79, 84; on "techne model of politics," 12, 80, 103, 106; terminology of, criticized as obscure, 42, 46; as theological, 61, 84; on thinking, from Catholicism to Protestantism, 77; thinking lauds Nietzscheanism, 77; thinking moves to gods and the holy, 77; on tragedy (and *Kampf*), 65, 66, 71, 75–76; on truth and *truthing*, 44, 46, 59, 64, 69; on will to power, xiii, 29–32, 37, 42–44, 47–50, 78–79, 86, 103; on world as created by creator, 79; and "worlding of world," 66, 68; and Zeus, 60, 61. *See also* beyng; *polemos*

Heidegger on being: and "Becoming," 31; on being (*des Sein/das Seyn*), xi, xvi, 12, 29–31, 35, 41–43, 46–48, 54; on being

M

Marion, Jean-Luc, xi

Marx, Karl, 94, 101, 119n16

Marxism, xvi, 97, 119nn16, 18; *Gestell*
 framework of controllability for, 103;
 Judeo-Christian ethic and, xiv, xviii,
 101, 102; as kind of Christianity, 94,
 101; and hyper-Christianity, xviii;
 nonrational, 94; postmodern, 100–103;
 violence in, 100, 101, 102–103

mediator: Christ as, 54; Heidegger on poet's
 exile as, 71; Logos as, 57; *mesistes* as,
 54, 55, 57

mercy, 6; over sacrifice, 110n14; virtue of,
 110n15

meta-metaphysical philosophy
 (mindfulness), 75

metanarratives: Girard on, xiv, 1, 11, 106;
 mistrust of, xii–xiv, 11, 106; truth as, 11

meta-physical, 11, 34; forms, 10; Heidegger
 on human as, 47; Nietzsche on world
 as, 96

metaphysical desire, 3, 92, 93

metaphysical transcendence, 44–45, 48

metaphysics: beyng concealed in, 45, 47, 49;
 blasphemes God, 90; Christian, xviii;
 and Christianity's foundation, xv;
 definition of, x, 93; and Heidegger, xi,
 xiii, 14, 29, 43–49, 58, 76–77, 93, 100,
 116n47; Judeo-Christian ethic coupled
 with, xviii; of modern technology,
 78; of Nietzsche, 93; "nothing" (*das
 Nichts*) grounds, 45; onto-theo-
 logical, 84; overcoming, ix, xi, 47; as
 Platonism, ix, 33, 107n1 (Intro.); of
 presence, 53, 80, 100, 104; quiddity/
 whatness/essence inquiries of, 43;
 reductionism of, 47, 74; splitting the
 world, xi, xv, 33, 93; theology equated
 with, 114n28; and victims, xviii;
 violence caused by, 93; Western, xi; will
 to power in, 47, 49–50, 51, 78

Metaphysics (Aristotle), 58, 82, 84

meta ta phusika (meta-physics/metaphysics),
 as beyond the physical, 34, 43, 45

metatruth, xiv

mimesis: conflict and violence result from,
 3; human capacity for, 2; reflexive, 62,
 63; *skandalon* (obstacle) to, 3, 8, 9, 37

mimetic desire, 1, 108nn45; bad, 10;
 definition of, 92; on desire from
 within, 2; and Girard on *the first stone*,
 111n40; of God, 92–93; ideology of,
 28; *imitatio Christi* as, 93; as imitative,
 2; leads to violence, 3; as metaphysical,
 3, 92, 93; and meta-physical forms
 imitating, 10; and mimetic rivalry,
 92; physical as bad, 10, 92; in Plato's
 "mimetic ontology," 10; resentment as
 form of, 28; and rivalry, 10–11, 92; and
 who desires, 3; as will to power and
 ideology of Girard, 28, 32, 37

mimetic ethics, and *imitatio Christi*, 9, 11,
 86, 93

mimetic *polemos*, as Heidegger's artwork, 63

mimetic rivalry: bad kind of desire leads
 to, 10–11, 92; ending of, 9–10, 87; and
 eo ipso corruption, 112n44; Girard
 on, 3, 5, 7, 29, 37, 92, 108n5; imitative,
 13; of model becoming obstacle, 29,
 87; Platonic, 10, 90; in religion, 87;
 Satan as personification of, 8; violence
 reduces meaning of being, 87–88

mimetic theory (of Girard): and Augustine's
 insights, 89; as cause of violence, 1, 2; as
 essence of human nature, 1; and ethics
 of *imitatio Christi*, 9, 11, 86, 93; Girard
 on, xvi; and "good mimesis," 112n44;
 as imitating divine ideas, 87, 91; on
 mimesis breeding rivalry, 106; and
 mimetic desire, 1, 108n5; as opposed to
 need, 3, 108nn3–4, 110n26; and rivalry,
 3, 29, 112n44; as root of violence, 2,
 108n5; truths of, 89; and unsolved
 problem of human violence, xiv; as
 without novelty, 89

mimetic violence, 28, 63; and frenzy, 37; and
 will to power, 37, 87

Mit-leid (compassion), 24

Mitleid (pity, compassion), 23, 25, 26

35–37; on overcoming resentment, 35;
on overturning Platonism and mimesis
itself, 36, 37; on persecution, cathartic
effect from, 22; "perspectivism" of,
18, 19, 96, 97; as philosopher, 16, 18,
21; and Platonism's cultural death, 13;
postmodernism of, 93, 94–98; proto-
Freudian manner of, 22; reductionism
of, 47; religious hermeneutics of, 15,
113n3, 114n26; reputation of, 15; on
ressentiment, 19, 28–29, 33, 34, 44, 93,
99, 113n8; reverse Platonism of, xiii, 34,
107n1 (Intro.); sides with mythic, 15;
on suicide of science, 96; on suffering
theism under guise of modern science,
94; as theologian, 15, 16, 21; and
theology, 34; and theory of dual, split
world, 33, 35; *Thus Spoke Zarathustra*,
33, 34; on truth, xvi, 11, 36, 95–96; "The
Twofold Nietzschean Heritage," 16;
and Übermensch, 28, 37, 78; "versus
the Crucified," 33, 113n3; *Will to Power*,
17, 18, 20, 30, 32, 35; on will to power,
35–36, 92; on will to power creating
values to overcome, 19, 30, 32, 36, 94;
on will to power disguised as nobility,
29
Nietzsche on "becoming," 29, 31, 32, 35, 36,
37
Nietzsche on "being," xvi, 29, 35, 36, 47
Nietzsche on Christianity: on Christianity's
compassion and concern for victims,
15, 23–25, 26, 35; and Christianity's
suffering rejected by, 19–21, 23; on
conscience and guilt, 21, 22; critiqued
by, 23, 26; and "Crucified"/crucified
persons, 17, 26, 33, 38, 91; on cruelty,
21, 22, 32; and "death of God," 13, 96;
on denied substitutionary atonement
model, 26; and Dionysian Christianity
as unique, 15, 16, 17, 18, 20, 26–28, 33;
on God as pagan, 26–27; on guilt
sacrifice, 26; on individualism as
Christian virtue, 101; on Jesus and love,
27, 28; as Platonism, 15, 33; as religion

of weak, 19, 23; on sacrifice as necessity,
15, 18, 26, 101; on sacrifice of individual,
15, 18, 20–22, 26, 101
Nietzsche on metaphysics: critiqued by, 33;
and Eternal Return, 29, 35; and God
of, 34, 95; as metaphysician, 29, 32, 95;
and metaphysics as *metata-phusika*, 34,
43, 45; and metaphysics as Platonism,
ix–xi, 11, 33, 34; and overcoming, xi, 15,
29, 33, 48
Nietzsche on violence, 11, 16–18, 21, 22,
26, 32–33; and Dionysian violence
reaffirmation, 18, 20, 24, 32–33, 35,
37; on mimesis of, 37; as necessity
to sacrifice, and cruelty, 32; and
nonviolence, 15, 27; and revenge, 33–35,
44; on scapegoating, 15, 22, 32; and
victims, 23, 33; and violent sacred, 16,
22; and will to power, as essence or
violence, xiii, 20, 23, 28–34, 42–51,
78–79, 86–87, 97, 103
"Nietzsche versus the Crucified" (Girard),
19, 33, 113n3
nihilism, xvi; of Christianity, 27, 98; and
compassion, 25; definition of, 105,
106; Girard on postmodern, 103,
105, 106; and God's death, 50; as
Nietzscheanism, 49; as Nietzsche's
ascetic ideal, 19, 95, 96; Vattimo on,
103, 105
nonrational: concealed behind rational, 94;
conditions, xiii
nonviolence, of Christ, 112n41; Girard and,
15
nothing (*das Nichts*), 45, 46
"nothingness" 25, 108n6

O

obstacles: insurmountable (*skandalon*), 3, 8,
9, 28, 37; surmountable, 37
Oedipus, 5, 108n5, 109n10; and guilt and
evil, 3, 54
Oedipus at Colonus (Sophocles), 109n10
Oedipus Rex (Sophocles), 54, 109n10
On the Genealogy of Morals (Nietzsche), 16,